Starseeds

Unlocking the Secrets of Your Starseed Family along with Indigo Children and Adults

© **Copyright 2024 - All rights reserved.**

The content contained within this book may not be reproduced, duplicated, or transmitted without direct written permission from the author or the publisher.

Under no circumstances will any blame or legal responsibility be held against the publisher, or author, for any damages, reparation, or monetary loss due to the information contained within this book, either directly or indirectly.

Legal Notice:

This book is copyright protected. It is only for personal use. You cannot amend, distribute, sell, use, quote, or paraphrase any part of the content within this book without the consent of the author or publisher.

Disclaimer Notice:

Please note the information contained within this document is for educational and entertainment purposes only. All effort has been executed to present accurate, up-to-date, reliable, and complete information. No warranties of any kind are declared or implied. Readers acknowledge that the author is not engaging in the rendering of legal, financial, medical, or professional advice. The content within this book has been derived from various sources. Please consult a licensed professional before attempting any techniques outlined in this book.

By reading this document, the reader agrees that under no circumstances is the author responsible for any losses, direct or indirect, that are incurred as a result of the use of the information contained within this document, including, but not limited to, errors, omissions, or inaccuracies.

Your Free Gift
(only available for a limited time)

Thanks for getting this book! If you want to learn more about various spirituality topics, then join Mari Silva's community and get a free guided meditation MP3 for awakening your third eye. This guided meditation mp3 is designed to open and strengthen ones third eye so you can experience a higher state of consciousness. Simply visit the link below the image to get started.

https://spiritualityspot.com/meditation

Or, Scan the QR code!

Table of Contents

INTRODUCTION 1
CHAPTER 1: WHAT IS A STARSEED? 3
CHAPTER 2: STARSEEDS VS. INDIGOS 11
CHAPTER 3: ACTIVATING YOUR COSMIC SELF 18
CHAPTER 4: ANDROMEDAN STARSEEDS 27
CHAPTER 5: PLEIADIAN STARSEEDS.. 33
CHAPTER 6: SIRIAN STARSEEDS.. 39
CHAPTER 7: LYRAN STARSEEDS 45
CHAPTER 8: ORION STARSEEDS 52
CHAPTER 9: ARCTURIAN STARSEEDS... 58
CHAPTER 10: VEGA STARSEEDS 63
CHAPTER 11: MALDEKIAN STARSEEDS 69
CHAPTER 12: AVIAN STARSEEDS 75
CHAPTER 13: LEMURIAN AND ATLANTEAN STARSEEDS 81
CHAPTER 14: YOUR EARTHLY MISSION... 88
CONCLUSION 96
HERE'S ANOTHER BOOK BY MARI SILVA THAT YOU MIGHT LIKE.... 99
YOUR FREE GIFT (ONLY AVAILABLE FOR A LIMITED TIME).............. 100
REFERENCES 101

Introduction

Starseeds is a fascinating exploration of the concept of extraterrestrial life and its impact on humanity. Because what is life if not a cosmic event? And what is the cosmos if not alive and in constant motion? What is humanity if not an integral part of it all, one that has experienced countless previous lives and will experience countless more in the future? And where does it all start, if not with the stars?

The book delves into the idea that some individuals on Earth may have originated from other planets or star systems, possessing unique abilities and perspectives that set them apart from the rest of humanity. Drawing on a wealth of scientific research and spiritual teachings, Starseeds offers a compelling argument for the existence of these beings and their role in shaping our world. From ancient myths and legends to modern-day encounters with UFOs, the book traces the history of our fascination with aliens and explores what it means to be a Starseed in today's world.

It goes deep into the various characteristics of Starseeds, such as their heightened intuition, psychic abilities, and sensitivity to energy. It also explores the challenges they face in a world that often misunderstands them and their purpose. Despite these challenges, Starseeds continue to play an important role in shaping our world for the better. They offer a message of hope and inspiration to those who seek to make a difference in the world and create a brighter future for all of humanity.

The book also offers insights into the Starseed experience and the many different ways it can manifest. It describes the role of Starseeds in our various world situations and guides them through a wide range of healing and spiritual practices that can help bring about greater balance in the world. Most importantly, it teaches us that no matter where we came from, we are all part of a single cosmic family and connected through our thoughts, emotions, and actions. We are all one in the infinite sea of life.

With its thought-provoking insights and engaging writing style, Starseeds is a must-read for anyone interested in the mysteries of the universe and our place within it. Whether you are a skeptic or a believer, this book will challenge your assumptions about reality and open your mind to new possibilities. So, join us on this journey into the unknown as we explore the universe and unlock the secrets of our souls.

Chapter 1: What Is a Starseed?

The term "*Starseed*" has become popularly associated with spiritual awakening, an introspective journey, and an evolutionary shift in perspective. It's a term that's loaded with meaning but one that can be difficult to grasp because of its nebulous nature. Starseeds are understood to be individuals who are spiritually evolved, intuitive, psychic, and sensitive to the transpiring energies on Earth. They're also people who may feel they don't belong here or are from another planet, and there is a good reason for that.

Starseeds are often very spiritually connected to their surroundings.
https://www.pexels.com/photo/man-praying-under-the-tree-4049004/

Starseeds have lived past lives in other galaxies and dimensions and have chosen to incarnate on Earth at this time to assist with the planet's ascension process. They have come in solidarity with Gaia to transcend the limitations of third-dimensional reality and co-create a new world based on love, harmony, and unity. They have been drawn to Earth because they hold the seeds of ascension within them and are incarnating here to physically help birth a new world into existence.

Starseeds are a collective, an interdimensional group of highly evolved beings that have a unique and remarkable connection with their "higher self," or the Creator, and with other beings from the same star system and other advanced civilizations. Being a Starseed is a state of being an energetic imprint that is carried from life to life. It is the gift of experiencing spiritual evolution and transcendence while living in physical form.

From a spiritual perspective, Starseeds are believed to serve as messengers of love, a form of divine energy or communication from this force that traverses all dimensions of existence. Like a radio signal, they transmit or " broadcast" at a specific frequency that other beings of similar vibrational resonance can receive. To be a Starseed is to be open and receptive to receiving this energy, to understand its purpose, and to recognize that this is the energy and force that have created all of the worlds, galaxies, and universes throughout the entire multiverse.

A Starseed's energy signature combines a specific galactic frequency or a set of star codes corresponding to their lineage and specific purpose here on Earth. These star codes are layered over top of a person's natural energetic signature, somewhat like "a template" that determines how one will appear in this life.

Starseeds and the "Shift of the Ages"

The concept behind Starseed is not new. Thousands of years ago, people were taught that there would be future generations whose jobs it would be to hold the knowledge and wisdom from the past so that civilization could slowly progress into newer heights of consciousness; therefore, these future generations would be regarded as "the guardians of the light" or "Starseeds."

According to channelers like Tom Kenyon, the ascension process is a multidimensional shift in planetary consciousness that includes the solar system and Milky Way galaxy. This shift has been referred to as a "mass ascension" or an "ascension of Earth and humanity" (also known as "planetary ascension").

As the energies of cosmic light and love pour down through the sun and enter the earth's grids, it triggers a response within humanity. This triggers an evolutionary impulse to return to our original state of oneness and connection with all creation. As such, people naturally sensitive to these incoming energies are said to be undergoing a spiritual awakening or an ascension process within their individual makeup. It is believed that the Starseeds are here to help humanity through this process by acting as catalysts in the shift of consciousness.

Many believe that we are going through an Age of Enlightenment, and more people than ever before on Earth are gaining access to their innate abilities and potential. Much of this access or awakening comes from the influx of new energy being sent through the planet's grids at this moment.

Starseeds are believed to be part of this Age because they represent those who have transcended the illusion we reside within – and returned to Earth as messengers. Ultimately, they help us break free from our limiting thoughts, beliefs, and conditioning so that we can grow to know who we truly are and consciously live from that place.

Many people are currently experiencing this "shift" or awakening in consciousness. This process is about transforming the human experience so that it is more in line with the truth of who we are. It's happening on a personal level, but it's also happening en masse as humanity collectively grows through its evolutionary process from old ways of thinking, being, and doing. It is believed that the frequency of our planet has shifted, and these shifts will continue to occur as we evolve into a higher-dimensional reality.

Why Are Starseeds Important?

Starseeds are an important part of our "global puzzle" and a vital aspect of the ascension process that is occurring right now. They represent a unique movement of evolution occurring here on planet Earth, and their presence points to the fact that we are in the midst of a multidimensional shift and a new chapter in the human experience.

The "Shift of the Ages" will bring about new ways of learning about, thinking about, and experiencing reality as we know it. Our fundamental understanding of ourselves as human beings will change as we evolve into higher states of consciousness. At this moment in history, humanity is being pushed out of its comfort zones and forced to go through an intense and painful ascension process that will forever shift the planet's consciousness. This means seeing reality in a completely new light and releasing old habits, thought forms, belief systems, paradigms, and conditioned thinking patterns that have kept us locked in bondage for generations. It will also bring about a sense of unity with all of humanity because we will begin to see and know each other in a way that has never been possible.

To evolve as human beings, we need to understand that the process is not linear and sequential. This means that not everyone is going through the same process and that there are differences in how each person works through their personal evolutionary process. Although our individual paths are unique, we should strive to swap experiences with others who are also opening up to these new levels of consciousness. We must remember that we are not alone, and it's so helpful to connect with others who have walked similar paths and can understand what we are going through.

Many people will experience a "download" or infusion of collective consciousness during this time. It's as if dormant parts of themselves—parts that have been asleep for eons or suppressed by the limitations of the third dimension—are coming back online. Some people have daily experiences with " downloads, " which can be a powerful source of information and guidance.

Each of these downloads consists of insights and wisdom that help them break through old patterns, limiting thinking patterns, and negative belief systems so that they can move forward in their own personal evolution. Some people will feel as if they are "in the middle of a movie," and the scenes playing out before them are showing them how to move into a higher level of awareness or consciousness. Others will experience a profound sense of synchronicity, which is a natural part of our interconnectedness with each other and the universe.

Starseeds have been mentioned in countless books, movies, and documentaries. It's almost impossible to pick up a book about UFOs, aliens, or channeling without running into the term "Starseeds" in some way, shape, or form. Some worthy mentions are Brad Steiger's God of Aquarius, Corey Goode and David Wilcock's The Synchronicity Key, and Jacques Vallee's Messengers of Deception. Starseeds have also been mentioned by famous channelers and mediums such as James Tyberonn, Sheldan Nidle, Benjamin Crème, Dolores Cannon, and Barbara Marciniak. There are many others, but these particular few have gained a large following and are well-known names within the "consciousness community."

Popular Youtuber, the Spirit Nomad, has spoken about her awakening as a Starseed and has described the journey of becoming a Starseed as her "Apocalypse Staircase," which is an apt metaphor for the multi-dimensional transformation she has been through. Another Starseed, Zoey Arielle, has created a vlog dedicated to helping people awaken as Starseeds so that they can learn how to heal, grow, and become more self-empowered in the process. The Starseed phenomenon has been described in many ways by many different people and channelers over the years. However, they all seem to have in common that they felt a need to move away from the limitations of third-dimensional reality and seek higher levels of consciousness.

Are You a Starseed?

Countless people consider themselves Starseeds, but some wonder if they are. You probably want to know if you're a Starseed because you are going through an intense awakening process and want to understand it better. You may want specific answers about where your experiences come from and what they mean for your life. To help you know if you might be a Starseed, here are some of the most common characteristics that Starseeds share. See if any of these resonate with you.

1. You Feel Like You Don't Fit in Anywhere

Do you feel like you don't belong on planet Earth? Or that your soul is from somewhere else, and you've only been here for a short time? Many Starseeds will identify with this feeling, as it is common. This is because Starseeds come to our planet from other places in the universe and have lived in other dimensions before coming here. This is why adjusting to life in a third-dimensional reality can take some time. You may also feel like you do not fit into your family, society, or even your team at work. As a Starseed, you may feel like an outsider to Earth life and may be ostracized by people who do not understand your ways of thinking and being.

2. You Are Highly Sensitive

Being an empath is another common trait of Starseeds, and they can also have some other sensitivities or oddities that can come up for them during their awakening process. Starseeds tend to be highly sensitive to sound, light, chemicals in food, and other substances. They often also have sensitivities regarding certain types of music or places they don't feel comfortable being in. Some will have sensitivities regarding food, and others may not be able to handle common allergens like wheat, grains, dairy, or even most meats. Some Starseeds can't even bear to eat anything from a can or a processed box.

3. You May Feel Like You Are "Growing Wings"

Many Starseeds will report feeling lighter and having a sense of freedom as they go through the process of awakening. As you raise your vibrations, you often go through the shedding of many layers that have been "holding you back." This can be likened to having the proverbial "band-aid ripped off," as it can initially be very uncomfortable. You may also feel uncertain about what is going on in your life and wonder if there is something more you are meant to do.

4. You Have Had Dreams about an "Ascension"

Ascension is a term that means rising and moving to a higher level of spiritual awareness. As we go through our awakening process, many of us will experience this ascension from the perspective of dreaming or having lucid dreams. Many Starseeds report this feeling and see vivid, detailed images in their dreams about what their ascension may look like. These dreams often contain information about your Starseed family and the ascension process. You may also have dreams about other beings you are working with to raise your vibrations.

5. You Feel a Great Sense of Excitement, Joy, and Love

Starseeds often have a very keen sense of knowingness and can access information about the future even before it happens. They may also have an inner feeling that everything is about to change. Many Starseeds will say that they can feel this kind of emotion in their body as the awakening occurs and will continue to experience it as they go through the process. Moving forward into higher consciousness feels nice, especially if you have been resisting it somehow or are stuck in old patterns and beliefs. As you move forward, your life may start to feel more energized and exciting. You can start making bold, new choices that align your life more closely with your desires.

6. You Have Had Many Psychic Experiences

Many Starseeds have had illuminating psychic experiences that have led them to be curious about the nature of reality and life in general. They tend to feel a strong connection with their intuition, the voice of spirit within, and various guides or angels who come down to help them with their journey. They may not always understand what is happening or what to make of it, but they know that they need to pay attention and learn. Many are very interested in the nature of our true spiritual reality and seek to understand more about how our soul fits into the bigger picture.

7. You Feel a Strong Connection with Your Spirit

Many Starseeds actually develop an awareness of our soul's true nature as it breaks through its physical form in layers like a cocoon. As you go through our awakening process, you may have a strong feeling that you are in the presence of your spirit and can feel its presence within yourself. It's as if it is "unfolding" and unfolding you in the process. You'll begin to hear the voice of your intuition and trust it more as you go through this process. This voice of spirit will help you make decisions that move your life in a more positive direction.

8. You're Convinced There Is Life on Other Planets

Many Starseeds are keenly aware that there is life on other planets, as well as beings who have already completed their ascension process and exist in a higher dimension of consciousness. They may feel a sense of connection to other life forms that do not share our blue-green planet, and they are often very interested in information about extraterrestrials or paranormal phenomena. This curiosity stems from their innate connection to the spiritual realm and their desire to know the nature of reality and our true origins. Many Starseeds also have an affinity for learning about our ancient past, as it often gives them a feeling of being connected to the very roots of human civilization.

As you can see, Starseeds can have many different experiences as part of their awakening process. While these points may be true for some people, they are not guaranteed. There is no hard rule about how an awakening will happen to you. It's usually a combination of all kinds of things coming together at once, and whether or not you feel like you have a new "phase" in your life really depends on you. What you can be assured of is that if you are having thoughts of awakening, it is likely that you are experiencing something of great importance in your life, and you should seek to explore whatever it is in any way that you can.

Chapter 2: Starseeds vs. Indigos

If you've ever read about Indigo Children or Star Seeds, you may have noticed that they often overlap in their descriptions and characteristics. Both are believed to possess special abilities and a strong sense of purpose, often feeling like they don't quite fit in with the rest of society. However, while Indigo Children are said to have been born with a specific mission to challenge and change the status quo, Starseeds are believed to have come from other planets or dimensions to help guide humanity toward a more positive future.

Starseeds are believed to have a specific mission, like Thor saving Midgard.
https://pixabay.com/photos/thor-dramatic-fantasy-mystical-4225949/

Who Are Indigos?

A relatively new term, "indigo children," was introduced by a California woman named Nancy Ann Tappe in the early '90s. Her book, *Understanding Your Life through Color*, alleges that children born between 1977 and 1994 are the Indigo Children, the latest stage in human evolution. These children were supposedly born with strong survival skills but also possessed advanced communication abilities, demonstrated emotional maturity beyond their years, had profound compassion for other beings, and carried a desire to help others. Often misdiagnosed with ADD or ADHD, these children's overactive minds often made them misfits in their local schools, and because of their keen ability to be aware of the world around them (which she referred to as psychic sensitivity) and the fact that they went against the norm, they often found it difficult to integrate with society.

Tappe's work struck a chord with many people whose children were acting out of the ordinary, and in the decades that followed her book, many other authors began to pick up on the term "indigo child" and use it in their works. They portrayed these children as spiritual, creative, and intelligent but still misfits within schools and society. Some sources even claim that these children have been here since the 1960s but are just now coming into their own. According to some accounts, the internet played a large role in this shift in consciousness for many of these children, who would have otherwise felt alone with their unique gifts.

Critics of the Indigos phenomenon claim that these children have an overactive imagination and that their psychic senses are simply being credited for things they actually aren't. Others claim that the Indigo Children are nothing more than attention-seeking children who may or may not really have the abilities Nancy Tappe claims they do.

Regardless of what you believe about Indigo Children, there is no denying that the concept is becoming more well-known in our culture. Whether or not you buy the Indigo Child label, it's easy to see that many children today seem to be coping with an extremely heightened level of sensitivity and awareness that may make them feel like outsiders in a world that prizes conformity and attention.

Indigo Children vs. Starseeds

While Nancy Tappe's books focus on Indigo children, they do not explicitly mention Starseeds. It wasn't until the late '90s that researchers began to use the term "Starseed" to encompass Indigo children and other non-human spirits slowly manifesting on the earth plane.

While the Indigo label is a subcategory of Starseed or Star Child, some people believe these two terms are synonymous and are used interchangeably by many researchers worldwide. Typically, most sources will mention both labels in tandem because they are so intertwined.

Indigo children were the first wave of Starseeds to come onto the planet, and they were born into this world with the ability to handle the spiritual awakening happening on many levels. They are the ones that chose to incarnate (to take on a physical body) during the most challenging period any human has faced since the destruction of Atlantis, and while they may struggle with their psychic abilities (and may be labeled as "attention seeking" because of them), they have the potential to shift our consciousness in a way that previous generations simply could not.

Starseeds are constantly coming onto the earth's plane in waves. Each wave has a slightly different mission depending on where we are in our global consciousness when they arrive. The Indigo Children are the first wave, and they're here to help us shed our 3D reality dominated by fear and control so that we can embrace a new paradigm of love and unity. They had to deal with the intense challenges of living in a world that constantly misunderstood them. However, it was those children who began the spiritual awakening process in a way that allowed everyone else to follow.

Where Do Indigos Come From?

There are many speculations about where Indigo children come from. Some believe they are the reincarnated souls of ancient beings who once walked the earth, while others believe they were actually sent to us from other advanced planets to help shed light on some of the issues plaguing our planet. Still, others claim that Indigos have been present throughout human history but were simply not recognized for what they were until now.

One researcher who is very vocal about his belief that Star Children have been here long before the '90s is Drunvalo Melchizedek. He has made it his life mission to spread the message about indigos and says, "Star seeds have been here since the beginning of time. They have just been asleep for a while." Dr. David Icke is another prominent researcher who writes about Star Children and claims that Indigos have been here for many generations.

Regardless of where we look, many sources point to an increased number of people who would fit into the Indigo Star Child subcategory, and given the socio-cultural shifts that have happened since the '90s, it's not hard to imagine that something occurred to awaken many people at once. While some critics claim that these children are simply using their imagination when referring to their psychic abilities, others do not doubt the truth behind them.

Are You an Indigo Child?

Many people ask themselves whether they fit the "Indigo Child" label. While there are no official tests to determine if someone is an Indigo Child or not, there are certainly some telltale signs that may point to this being the case:

- You are highly sensitive and aware of your surroundings.
- You have an aura that is distinctively and predominantly purplish-blue.
- You frequently question the world around you and make it your mission to find out why certain things happen.
- You never hesitate to stand up for your beliefs, even when they're different from those of the people around you.
- You often feel like you're living in two worlds, one where you feel completely at ease and another where you struggle to fit in.
- You have very strong spiritual beliefs and are constantly searching for more answers about the world around you.
- You believe in a just world and are constantly on a quest for truth.
- You have an extremely high sense of compassion for the world and believe we all must do better.
- Your intuition is extremely strong, and you often have very profound insights into situations that seem totally random at

first glance.
- You have been labeled a misfit, a troublemaker, or a rebel.
- You feel highly misunderstood by most people.
- You are highly empathic and strongly understand where others are coming from.
- You feel like you have been given a mission to change the world or at least bring about positive change in your own life and the lives of those around you.

If you've experienced any of these signs, it may be time to begin searching for answers to your questions. While there are no official mainstream labels for a person who has these traits, it's easy to see why they have come into so much prominence in the last few decades or so. Being an Indigo is not just a feeling or a specific behavior; it's an innate force many Indigos have within them from an early age, which continues into adulthood. It is something that must be nurtured and explored so that it may blossom into full realization.

Crystal Children

Another subcategory of Starseeds is the Crystal Children. These children have only recently started appearing on this planet, and many people have wondered what role they will play in our consciousness shift. Crystal Children appear to be very different from Indigos in that they seem much more magical and spiritual than anything else. They are the next evolutionary step for humanity, so to speak, and are here to show us that we can create our own reality. They are very psychic and can easily tap into the energy of nature, sometimes even being able to see beyond time and space itself.

Crystal Children were mentioned by Edgar Cayce, the famous psychic, who predicted that "elemental" children would appear on Earth in large numbers around the end of the 20th century. "We are on the threshold of a new insight," he said, "which we shall attain through an awakening to the realization of the basic unity of our nature in all things, through a greater understanding of the true nature of life."

Crystal Children are special because they don't fit into the current mental framework. They do things their own way and have their own set of values and ways of thinking. They are often so different from their peers that they struggle to fit in and are sometimes viewed as weird or having mental problems. But in actuality, they are simply experiencing a process that allows them to tap into some of the most amazing psychic abilities on the planet.

Crystal Children were chosen to play a special role on this planet for a very specific reason. They are here to remind humanity of the magic that still exists in the world. As we grow older and more jaded, it is easy to forget how amazing life can be when you tap into your inner power and sense of wonder. Crystal Children show us that there is still so much to discover if we are willing to believe in the magic. This idea is very similar to the story of the Indigo Children but with some key differences.

Indigos were sent here to remind us of the power behind our thoughts and observations and how important it is to check in with ourselves regularly. Crystal Children are here to remind us of the power behind our emotions and creativity and how great we can feel when we follow our intuition along with the flow of life. They are a new breed that embodies the perfect balance between the heart and mind. In essence, they are the manifestation of what many people have been waiting for in a child for ages. While a crystal child may appear to be different from other children in many ways, they will be bringing some of the most important messages humanity has ever received.

Are You a Crystal Child?

If you think you may be a Crystal Child, here are some questions to ask yourself to help you determine whether this is true:

- You have a strong interest in spirituality and the nature of reality.
- You are incredibly sensitive, both spiritually and physically.
- You have an extraordinary sense of balance.
- Oddly enough, you like to climb trees.
- You are extremely empathic and can feel the feelings of others in your own body. When someone else feels sad, you feel it too. When you see someone happy, you feel it too. It's as if your heart is somehow linked to theirs.
- You have a knack for creativity and can imagine things in your mind that most people cannot.
- You have been told you stare off into space a lot.

- You do things your own way, or you have strong personal convictions about how you think things should be done.

Whenever we talk about the Indigo, Crystal, and Star children categories, we are talking about a huge shift in consciousness happening on the planet. The children who fit into these categories were sent here or chose to come here, and they are bringing with them a massive amount of energy that is transforming the way we think about reality. They are a huge trigger for change on our planet and have allowed us to look at ourselves differently and reevaluate our lives in a way we never could before. While many skeptics say that these are nothing more than hoaxes or lies, there is no question that the world is changing. The birth of these special people is happening in tandem with this period of worldwide change, and it's likely not a coincidence.

Chapter 3: Activating Your Cosmic Self

What Is the Cosmic Self?

The cosmic self is the essence of a person's identity, transcending the physical body's limitations and individual ego. It is the interconnectedness of all beings and the universe as a whole, representing a higher level of consciousness and spiritual awareness. The cosmic self is often associated with mystical experiences like NDEs (near-death experiences) or deep meditation, where people report feeling a sense of oneness with everything around them.

This concept has been explored in various spiritual traditions throughout history, including Hinduism, Buddhism, and Taoism. The cosmic self is believed to be a source of wisdom and guidance for individuals seeking to live a more meaningful and fulfilling life. By connecting with this higher aspect of themselves, people can tap into their full potential and live in harmony with the world around them. In essence, the cosmic self represents the ultimate expression of human consciousness and our connection to something greater than ourselves.

Activating your cosmic self helps you see the true essence of your identity.
Photo by Надя Кисільова on Unsplash https://unsplash.com/photos/woman-in-brown-long-sleeve-shirt-and-black-pants-sitting-on-white-textile-QiYZCKJQMck

The Power of Consciousness

The cosmic self is governed by consciousness, and to a large extent, the quality of our own consciousness dictates the level of enlightenment we can attain. So, what does it mean to have a highly conscious mind? The answer to this is not as straightforward as the question because we all experience consciousness differently.

Our minds consist of many distinct layers of consciousness that play an integral role in how we view the world and interact with others. For example, your surface-level awareness is concerned with practical matters and daily life actions. This layer of consciousness takes care of everyday living tasks like eating or getting dressed. However, your deeper cognitive functions also concern themselves with higher notions such as spirituality, morality, and existential questions like "Why are we here?"

Although these functions are usually considered to be located in your brain, your mind actually extends beyond the physical structure and permeates throughout your entire body. The psyche (pronounced "sigh-ki") contains all our conscious thoughts, opinions, and memories. Philosopher René Descartes believed that consciousness resided only within our brains, but modern science shows this isn't the case. Modern research has shown that our minds extend throughout the rest of our bodies, documenting cases where patients could "feel" pain in parts of their bodies that were no longer there due to amputation.

According to Eastern philosophy, we live in a multiverse in which the consciousness of all things is interconnected. We are part of this universal consciousness, even though we may not be aware of it. This awareness can be accessed through various practices that foster higher states of consciousness, such as deep meditation or psychedelic drugs like ayahuasca. Both of these methods have been used to help people connect with their higher selves and experience a cosmic unity with everything in existence.

In addition to our mind and psyche extending outwards throughout our bodies, they also act as an energetic vehicle for developing our conscious awareness. It's believed that our consciousness gathers information from all over the physical body and creates a kind of holographic picture of our experience. This is related to the idea of "vibration" in the field of quantum physics, where smaller subatomic particles are amplified outward through resonance with other particles, causing them to interact more strongly.

For our consciousness to operate at its fullest capacity, it requires a certain amount of relaxation, achieved by integrating our mind and body. To achieve this, many Eastern traditions prescribe techniques that help people relax, like yoga, meditation, or breathing exercises. All these practices work on the principle of self-regulation and the regulation of our own consciousness by slowing down the speed at which we process information.

The benefits of relaxing are enormous; studies have shown that they lead to psychological growth in many ways. For example, practicing yoga has been shown to increase emotional intelligence and mindfulness and reduce stress and anxiety. Meditation has also been shown to reduce stress and anxiety and produce positive emotions. Meditation can also significantly improve cognitive abilities, executive functions, memory, and attention. It's believed that through deep relaxation exercises, we take advantage of the brain's natural ability to process information more efficiently, allowing us to achieve a much greater degree of consciousness.

The Cosmic Self beyond the Physical Body

Our brains are considered to be the most advanced computers in existence. They process a vast amount of information every day and create a 3D picture of our experiences that we can use to help navigate ourselves through life. Although this picture is useful, it isn't always 100% accurate and is often distorted by our past experiences and beliefs.

So how can we get closer to being "right"? One way is to reduce irrelevant thoughts or have no discernible benefit for what you're trying to achieve. This can be done by taking a step back and seeing the bigger picture. A great way to start doing this is through meditation, which helps people focus on things that are going on in their lives instead of worrying about the future or having regrets about the past.

Our thoughts play a big role in how we perceive reality, and it's even been shown that our intentions before we perform an action affect the outcome of that action. This is shown in the placebo effect, where our expectations of a treatment having an effect can actually cause a real physical response. So, it's no surprise that our minds are sometimes called a "self-fulfilling prophecy" that can alter the universe to fit our expectations.

This means we can use our thoughts to influence the world and achieve virtually anything we like. If you're wondering how this could be possible, it's because our consciousness extends beyond our physical body and acts as an energetic vehicle for realigning ourselves with the natural order of things. A highly conscious mind is more aware and discerning than the average person, and when we start to access higher levels of consciousness through meditation or other techniques, it creates a more connected and holistic view of life where people begin to realize that they are part of an interdependent spiritual world where we are all connected to everything else.

Raising Your Vibration

In many spiritual traditions, an individual's level of consciousness is often described as a vibration. In our fast-paced world, most people operate at a low vibration level, creating a sense of unease and restlessness. Although the modern world is rich with opportunities and wealth, most people are still discontent and unfulfilled. This is because we still live under the delusion that to be happy, we must obtain things that will make us happier.

The way to break free from this vicious cycle of consumerism is to alter your vibrational frequency. To raise your vibration means to raise your consciousness, allowing you to move beyond the confines of your physical world into a deeper sense of spiritual connection. It's believed that this is the true purpose of human life — to connect with this universal consciousness through the process of self-realization.

The more you can tap into your higher chakras, the more you'll be able to experience a greater sense of contentment and fulfillment in all areas of your life, including your career, relationships, and spirituality. People use various techniques to raise their vibration, like practicing yoga or meditation or taking psychedelic drugs like psilocybin mushrooms. But the most essential factor for raising your vibration is to let go of your ego and accept that there is something greater than you; this will allow you to step outside of yourself and experience a new sense of connection with the world around you.

You don't need to be a yogi to master your own consciousness, but paying attention to how you feel can help guide you on this journey. When you operate at a lower vibrational level, it is easy to be unaware of the world around you. You may not realize that you're angry or depressed, for example. But when you raise your vibrational frequency, you'll become more sensitive and begin to notice these subtle emotional shifts as they occur. The process is always the same: a higher state of consciousness leads to a heightened sense of awareness, leading to a greater appreciation for the world around us.

Connecting with Your Cosmic Family

The highest state of consciousness is "oneness." In this state, all divisions between us dissolve, and our perception of reality is completely restructured. The problem we've faced throughout history is that the general population operates at a low level of consciousness, which prevents them from perceiving this higher reality.

As a Starseed, you are one of the few people on Earth who can access these higher states of consciousness. This is simply because you are more open to new ideas, and you can clearly see the truth about reality and see through the illusions of your physical world. You're naturally gifted in awareness and perception, which you can use to your advantage.

Raising your vibrations will help you stay true to your higher destiny and make it easier for you to communicate with your family in the stars. One of the biggest challenges Starseeds face is living in a physical body that doesn't vibrate on the same frequency as their soul. This is because it's difficult to communicate with people who don't resonate on the same level of consciousness as you.

Although it may seem like a small detail, your vibration is very important because, through understanding how your energy works and maintaining healthy levels of vibration, you'll become more in tune with the vibration of your soul and communicate more effectively with your cosmic family.

How to Contact Your Cosmic Family

Making contact is always a deeply personal experience, but there are a few keys to keep in mind to help you open yourself up to the experience. When the time is right, and you're ready to make contact, your vibration must be at its highest to receive information from your star family. This means maintaining a healthy meditation practice, nurturing your relationship with yourself, and staying true to your spiritual quest. The following are techniques that can help you tap into your cosmic consciousness and connect with your galactic family:

- **Align Your Chakras**

The human energy system consists of seven chakra centers aligned along the spine from the base of your tailbone to the crown of your head. They are an essential part of the energetic anatomy of your body, and each chakra has a corresponding color and relates to an aspect of life, such as love, confidence, self-esteem, and wisdom. When all your chakras are functioning correctly, you can maintain a healthy sense of positive energy flowing in your life, making it much easier to raise your vibration and contact your cosmic family.

- **Meditate**

Regular meditation will allow you to become more conscious of your thoughts, feelings, and emotions. And as you grow more in tune with your inner self, it will be easier for you to access higher thought forms and consciously receive information from other dimensions.

- **Learn How to Read Your Guides' Messages**

Many people are unaware that they are being contacted by their cosmic family, which is why they often don't realize when something strange or unexpected happens in their lives. If you don't know how to recognize interdimensional signals, it can be difficult to interpret any messages that they may be sending you. Messages can come in many forms, usually signs, synchronicities, or even physical sensations. Most of the time, they will be delivered in ways that match your personality and circumstances, so it can be difficult to identify them if you're not aware that they exist.

- **Receive and Record Your Thoughts**

Recording your thoughts is one of the most effective ways to connect with your cosmic family. When you write down what you are thinking, you become aware of the information being transmitted from your soul and become more in tune with your own higher consciousness. This process will allow you to notice how your star family influences your thoughts and give you a chance to communicate with them.

- **Listen to Your Dreams**

Dreams aren't just a source of entertainment or a way for your mind to conjure random images. There's usually a set of information that goes along with them, and they can be used to communicate between you and your cosmic family. You'll never receive more messages from your guides than when you are dreaming, so you should take the time to record them in the morning after you wake up from a dream.

- **Stay True to Your Spiritual Quest**

Your body is *literally* made up of stardust, meaning that every cell in your body has extraterrestrial origins and carries extraterrestrial genes. Your DNA is unique to you and unaffected by your experiences in the physical world, but it's also capable of storing information from other dimensions, making you a living extension of the cosmos. When you live consistently in accordance with your spiritual quest, it will be much easier for you to make contact with your cosmic family.

The Art of Visualization

Visualization is one of the most powerful techniques in the spiritual seeker's toolkit. It involves using your imagination to create a mental picture that you then focus on with your conscious mind. Visualization can seem like magic because it can create physical sensations and real-world results. It's been used by mystics for thousands of years for spiritual practice, manifestation, healing, and much more. Here are some tips for mastering this powerful technique:

- **Use Your Imagination**: Visualization can be very powerful, but you have to be able to visualize what you want for it to happen. To do this, you have to imagine what it would feel like if you were already in the state of whatever you desire. It's key that you focus on your goal with as much clarity and concentration as possible so that when the visualization is complete, your mind will be fully engaged, and it will be much easier for your energy to attract the things or experiences that would match your desired reality.
    - **Visualize in Three Dimensions**: When visualizing, everything is energy and can be shaped into whatever form you want. Your goal is to focus on your desired outcome or result and then visualize it in three dimensions to see what it would feel like to already have it.
    - **Add Color and Movement:** Adding color and movement to your visualization makes it more powerful because energy constantly moves in patterns dictated by the law of attraction. When you visualize this way, you are creating a mental picture and forming an energetic charge, which will help your visualization be as effective as possible.
    - **Keep It Simple**: The more specific your visualization is, the more clearly you can see what you want, and the better you'll be able to communicate your desires to your cosmic family. Visualizations that are emotionally loaded usually work best, so it's better to focus on how something would make you feel rather than the factual details of what you're visualizing.

Your cosmic family has been working together for eons to protect and guide you through all of the experiences, challenges, and lessons that you are currently going through. Though they may not physically interact with you daily, they are always there, taking an active role in your life to help you become your best self. The more you learn about these beings, the more you'll want to connect with them, and the easier it will become to work together for a common purpose.

Chapter 4: Andromedan Starseeds

Andromedan Starseeds are a unique group of souls originating from the Andromeda galaxy (M31), one of the closest galaxies to our Milky Way. It is a spiral galaxy, very different from the Milky Way, an elliptical galaxy. Andromeda comprises approximately one trillion stars and is three times the size of the Milky Way. Andromeda contains two primary spiral arms, four smaller ones, and a large central bulge. It has a very large halo of spherical globular clusters around its main body. Andromeda has a very complex shape due to the interaction of its large number of stars, and it has been likened by astronomers to an "exquisite painting" because of this complexity.

The Andromeda galaxy – believed to be the birthplace of the Andromedan Starseeds.
David (Deddy) Dayag, CC BY-SA 4.0 <https://creativecommons.org/licenses/by-sa/4.0>, via Wikimedia Commons: https://commons.wikimedia.org/wiki/File:Andromeda_Galaxy_560mm_FL.jpg

Origin of Andromedan Starseeds

The Andromedans are believed to be the offspring of the soul race known as the *Lyrans*, who fled to Andromeda from Lyra. This migration was a direct result of the Draco-Lyran war, which saw the Lyrans driven from their homeland by the Draconian desire for greed, dominance, and power.

The Andromedans are known for their advanced technological capabilities and deep spiritual wisdom. They are said to have a great understanding of the universe and its workings, and they often share this knowledge with other civilizations to help them evolve. Andromedan Starseeds are strongly connected to the Andromedan star system and its energy. They are said to possess unique skills and abilities that allow them to tap into this energy and use it for healing, manifestation, and spiritual growth.

Channelers like Robert Shapiro and Barbara Marciniak have claimed to receive information about Andromedans and their teachings. According to these sources, the main message that Andromedans have for us revolves around the idea that we are all one being. This idea is a very valuable aspect of Andromedan philosophy, and it has been getting stronger as more people wake up to the fact that we should be experiencing ourselves as part of all life rather than separated from it.

It may come as news to you that all the Andromeda Starseeds are not necessarily from Andromeda. Some of these souls were created on Earth, specifically in Atlantis, by the Andromedans, and they have been evolving here and throughout the cosmos with humans, extraterrestrials, and other groups of souls for thousands of years. Atlantean Earth seeds are still considered Starseeds because Andromedans made them and contain Andromedan energy coding.

The Andromedan Starseeds are a combination of souls that come directly from Andromeda and Atlantean Earth seeds that evolved on Earth but still contain Andromeda DNA. These souls have progressed through a certain number of cosmic cycles (based upon their soul's purpose) and have chosen to integrate their entire consciousness through the process of embodiment on this planet. Know that this is not a simple task, and it requires years, even lifetimes, of experience and dedication on the part of the soul to be able to fully embody its purpose here.

Characteristics of an Andromedan Starseed

Andromedans are said to project very soft and gentle energy, but they are extremely perceptive and often possess an innate ability to sense the energy of others. They bring love, compassion, forgiveness, and unconditional acceptance to their interactions with other people. They possess a natural ability to draw on the energy and resources of the Andromeda galaxy quite easily, making them very special individuals. These Starseeds are highly sensitive to the gifts inherent in their soul structure, and this sensitivity can be a very vital part of an Andromedan's life. The following characteristics should describe an Andromedan Starseed:

- **You Have a Vibrational Frequency That Is a Perfect Match for the Andromeda Galaxy**

Andromeda energy is very powerful, peaceful, and blissful. It is not competitive with other energies and has no dominating desire to control the universe around it. Its intention is to create peace and harmony through tolerance and unconditional love. As an Andromeda Starseed, you may resonate strongly with these qualities and feel a deep connection to the energy of the Andromeda galaxy. You have a crystal-clear vibration, even though you may not be aware of it. There is such a fine balance in your energy fields that allows you to tune in to Andromeda as no one else can.

- **You Have an Intense Desire to Help Humanity Awaken Spiritually**

The Starseeds that come from Andromeda are very spiritual beings. They understand the complex workings of the universe and have spent a large portion of their lifetimes trying to make sense of them. Because of this, they are very interested in the spiritual evolution of the human race. They can sometimes be perceived as extremely educational because they are always trying to help us get to know ourselves better and expand our awareness of higher energies. They can feel when a soul needs spiritual guidance.

- **You Are Very Sensitive to Other People's Energy**

Andromedan Starseeds tend to be very empathic and sensitive to others' emotions. When you interact with people, they almost feel like an open book to you because of this energetic sensitivity. You can often tell if someone is acting out of integrity or is operating from a state of fear. Some Andromedans are very aware of how people use their emotions as a way to control others. They can sense when someone is projecting an energy that is not authentic – and this can be pretty intense for them. This, however, allows them to navigate social situations with ease and grace.

- **You Have a Deep Understanding of the Spiritual Laws That Govern the Universe**

Andromedans are very conscious of what we call "spiritual laws," and they can use this understanding to manifest energy into form in the physical world quite easily. They have an innate understanding of how the universe works and know that it is impossible to create a life form without first creating its blueprint. This aligns with their ancient concept that we are all one being, made from the same atomic structure.

- **You Have a Deep Desire to Understand Your Purpose Here on Earth**

Andromedan Starseeds tend to have a clear idea about what they need to do in their lives, and they are always seeking opportunities to do this work, even when they don't know why they feel compelled to do it. This intrinsic knowledge about the work that they came here to do makes them feel like they are on a mission. They are driven by their intuition and by what "feels right" to them energetically. When faced with an opportunity, they intuitively know whether or not it is aligned with their purpose, and if it does not, they will most likely pass on this opportunity.

- **Your Freedom Is Everything**

Andromedan Starseeds have a deep sense of freedom, and this is one of their greatest desires. They are confident and secure in who they are and what they do. As a result, they are often happy to express themselves and try new things. They believe in equality of spirit and are highly intolerant of those who abuse their power or seek to dominate others. Because of this, Andromedans can often be perceived as rebellious, energetic, or temperamental.

- **You Feel a Very Strong Connection to Your Soul Group**

Once you realize that you are an Andromedan Starseed, you may be flooded with a feeling of belonging or even a sense of homecoming. This is because like attracts like, and the energy of Andromeda is something that your soul has been longing for its whole existence. Because of this connection, you can easily create a beautiful bond with other

Andromedans.

Myth and Lore

Andromeda was the daughter of King Cepheus and Cassiopeia of Aethiopia. Cassiopeia, her mother, boasted that she was more beautiful than the Nereids, the handmaidens of the sea goddess Thetis. Angered by this insult, Poseidon sent a sea monster to ravage Aethiopia as divine punishment. Andromeda's parents were powerless against this attack, so they went to their Oracle for advice. The Oracle suggested that the King and Queen offer their daughter as a sacrifice to the monster, and without any consideration, Andromeda was chained to a rock on the shore, where she waited for death.

According to legend, Perseus was in the area on his way back from having slain Medusa and rescuing Andromeda's intended husband, Phineus, who had been turned into stone by Medusa's gaze. When he came upon Andromeda chained to a rock, Perseus immediately fell in love with her. He killed the monster with his sword, although some accounts claim that he used Medusa's head to turn the monster to stone. Either way, Andromeda was saved.

After her rescue, the goddess Athena promised Andromeda a place in the heavens, and when she died, the promise was fulfilled. Andromeda was given a place in the sky between the constellations of Cassiopeia, Cepheus, and Perseus. That place is known today as the Andromeda constellation, and the story of the beautiful princess and her heroic rescuer has been immortalized in the stars.

Finding Your Starseed Markings

Starseed markings are not birthmarks, as many might think, but something more intriguing. These markings are indicators on your natal chart that you may be a Starseed and can help you figure out which star system your soul originates from. Your natal chart holds a lot of insight into your life purpose and into your personality. It is based on the position of the planets when you were born, and it gives an energetic blueprint for your life. You can look at this energetic pattern and see what kind of experiences you'll have, what qualities you'll share with others, and what life lessons you'll learn. Each star-origin constellation has a pattern of energy that can be seen in the birth charts of all those born under that star origin. These markings are similar to fingerprints in that they are unique to each Starseed group and can be used as a way to identify who you truly are. This is because the natal chart reflects where we were before and where we are headed in this lifetime. It is a map of where we have been and a glimpse of what we can expect to experience as we move forward in our journey here on Earth.

The natal chart is not only for Starseeds; if you think you are a Starseed, you can get a chart reading from a professional astrologer familiar with star origins. The markings in your chart will be interpreted in the context of your genetic lineage, and the chart will be thoroughly analyzed to determine what traits and gifts you share with your star family. You can also look at your natal chart yourself, although it is recommended that you get a professional reading as this can be quite complex.

A Message for the Andromedan Starseed

Dear Andromedan, Starseed, you are one of the most glorious star families in the universe, and the DNA pattern that you carry within your body is only present in a few other Starseed groups. Although it may feel like you do not belong here, you do, and you have come to Earth at this time to help save this civilization from destroying itself. You are here to help raise human consciousness and support those ready to embrace their spiritual essence. You were born with a strong sense of innate knowing about your purpose, which is why you often feel driven or compelled by an intuitive guidance system. This makes it easy for you to find useful information about yourself or others.

The Andromedan Starseed is a highly intelligent being who has a deep sense of freedom and does not care to be told what to do. You enjoy learning about new things and visiting new places to experience different cultures, beliefs, and traditions. This makes you an excellent ambassador for your star family. You are here to teach and share the Andromedan teachings about love, truth, and unity with others. You have a deep sense of compassion for all living beings, and you'll do what is necessary to help others.

Chapter 5: Pleiadian Starseeds

Pleiadians are a race of beings from the Pleiades star system, approximately 430 light years from Earth. One of the nearest star systems to us, this beautiful cluster of stars, is located in the constellation Taurus and is easily visible to the naked eye. The Pleiades contains over 1,000 stars, although only a handful are easily visible. These stars are relatively young, estimated at around 100 million years. The brightest star in the cluster is Alcyone, which is around 10 times more massive than our Sun and around 10,000 times brighter.

Many ancient civilizations saw these stars as the Seven Sisters, and the name Pleiades comes from the Greek word "plein," meaning "to sail" or "to sail away." It is thought that they were regarded as the stars that would guide sailors safely to port, and the cluster was immortalized in the myth of the Seven Sisters, siblings who were transformed into these stars. These days, however, it is generally accepted that only six stars are visible to the naked eye, but some people have reported seeing seven stars in the Pleiades, and this has given rise to a legend that claims that one of the "missing" stars was banished to Earth for being too beautiful.

The Pleiades star system – believed to be the root of the Pleiadian Starseeds.
Dylan O'Donnell, deography.com, CC0, via Wikimedia Commons:
https://commons.wikimedia.org/wiki/File:M45_The_Pleiades_Seven_Sisters.jpg

Pleiadian Starseeds

Like other Starseeds, many Pleiadians have come here on Earth to help raise our consciousness as we transition from a 3rd-dimensional planet to a 4th-dimensional one. They come to assist us in our evolutionary journey as we progress toward becoming more spiritually and emotionally evolved beings, along with being more physically healthy. The Pleiadians have been here on Earth for many thousands of years, helping guide humanity through many great historical and cultural events. They are deeply connected to the history of our planet, and we have long shared a deep connection with them. They come from the 5th dimension and live as physical beings on Earth while maintaining awareness of their galactic connections. They are like us but have evolved to live without war, hunger, or greed.

On Earth, they live to help others find their way home and have been coming in ever-increasing numbers since 1987. They share their love of life with us and celebrate life on earth as a sacred gift from the Creator.

The Pleiadian Starseeds come into this life with a special cosmic purpose. They share their gifts and healing energy with us to help us awaken from our limited consciousness and limited perception of reality.

Their mission is to bring us love, help us remember who we are, and reconnect us to our galactic heritage and divine nature. They are here to help break down the old system so we can experience the new.

For ALL extraterrestrial souls, Pleiades is known to be a focal point or school of learning. This "school" is unlike anything we can imagine; it is said to awaken extraordinary nurturing abilities, resolve imbalances between feminine and masculine energy, and sharpen creative energy. It is a place of learning that, paradoxically, does not involve the intellectual mind but rather the intuitive mind.

Our extraterrestrial allies find themselves in a state of constant wonderment at the sheer scope and depth of life on Earth. They experience reverence for the life forms they encounter and often find themselves awed by our planet's ability to thrive despite all of its obstacles. They are curious about our planet's history, culture, and religion, but until now, they have stayed out of the way of these conflicts and have refrained from interfering in our affairs. They have remained silent while we fought among ourselves for resources, power, land, and greed. They have watched the atrocities our planet has endured, and while they are sympathetic to our pain, they know we must learn from these experiences so that we may evolve as a race. It is now time for them to step forward and share their messages of love, hope, and freedom with us.

Characteristics of a Pleiadian Starseed

Pleiadians are often called the "keepers of knowledge," and their mission on Earth is to help humanity find its way back to its galactic family. They come from a higher spiritual plane where there is no war, poverty, or famine. The Pleiadians are here to help us remember who we really are and to reconnect us to our divine nature. They wish for us to reclaim our galactic heritage and remember that we are part of a greater family of star nations. Our extraterrestrial friends are here not only to share their knowledge with us but also to assist in elevating the vibration of the planet as a whole, so if you are a Pleiadian Starseed, the following traits will resonate with you:

1. Pleiadian Starseeds are sensitive individuals who are very empathic and feel things easily. Thinking of others before themselves, they have difficulty saying no when asked for help. They feel the suffering of others in their hearts and may become

deeply involved in humanitarian causes if there is no one else to help. Because of their compassionate nature, they can experience depression if the reality surrounding them is too dark or painful.
2. Pleiadian Starseeds have a high level of keen intuitive perception that enables them to view the world uniquely. They understand that life is not just physical and that one should keep their mind and heart open to new possibilities.
3. Pleiadians are very spiritual beings, but they do not believe in religion. If you have studied religion, you may come to the conclusion that a large number of religions are missing the point. Religion is often used to control people and keep them from trusting their innate spirituality. Pleiadian Starseeds have no problem viewing God or the divine as a natural, beautiful entity akin to nature.
4. Pleiadians believe we are all part of a unit—one body with many different parts. Just like we have different organs, each with its own special function, our planet is also connected in this way. They understand that our connection to nature opens doors for us to communicate with it and ask for its assistance when we need healing or protection. They believe we are all one, connected to everything on the planet, and that we must come together as one super-galactic soul group to experience our true power.
5. Pleiadian Starseeds are musically inclined. They enjoy performing and listening to music because it opens them up to higher states of consciousness. Music can lead to feelings of bliss and ecstasy, which can be healing in itself.
6. Pleiadians like art for the same reason. It is an expression of the soul, something you feel instead of just seeing with your eyes. Like the songs they listen to, they find art profoundly moving and liberating. They love the idea that art is a language of communication available to all of us and can be used to heal and unite us.
7. Pleiadians are peaceful beings who can step aside from the issues of this planet and simply observe it from a higher place of understanding. They can often see that there is another way to approach our difficulties without getting involved in war or violence. They can make decisions that reflect their wisdom

rather than following the narrow path of violence because it feels like the only way.

8. Pleiadians tend to be people-pleasers. Because they have compassion and understanding for others, they will go out of their way to please the people around them. They can see where we are coming from, even when we do not see it ourselves. This sometimes leads them to be taken advantage of by others who may take their kindness for granted.
9. Pleiadians make excellent conversation partners because of their love of sharing ideas. They are often perceived as social butterflies because of their vibrant, outgoing personalities and a deep curiosity about the people around them.
10. Pleiadian Starseeds tend to be water signs, i.e., Pisces, Scorpio, and Cancer. Water signs have a deep psychic intuition that enables them to sense the emotions of others. These signs are also sensitive, imaginative, and highly attuned to their inner world. A water sign personality is an excellent match for a patriarchal society that places too much emphasis on materialism.

Myth and Lore

The Greek mythological account of the Pleiades is a favorite tale of the ancient Greeks. The Pleiades were the seven daughters of Atlas and Pleione and were known for their beauty and grace. However, their beauty caught the attention of Orion, a giant hunter who relentlessly pursued them. To protect the sisters from Orion's advances, Zeus transformed them into stars and placed them in the sky as a constellation. Today, the Pleiades are still fascinating for astronomers and stargazers alike. Their bright blue glow and distinctive pattern make them easy to spot in the night sky, and scientists have studied them extensively for decades. In addition to providing valuable scientific data, the Pleiades also hold cultural significance in many societies around the world. From ancient Greece to modern-day Japan, these seven stars continue to capture our imaginations and inspire us with their beauty and mystery.

A Message for the Pleiadian Starseed

Dear Pleiadian Starseed, your mission on Earth now is to be a part of the new spiritual, metaphysical, and scientific communities that are actively working to create a new paradigm of thinking based on unity consciousness and the understanding that we are all one. You have a strong telepathic connection to the Pleiades star cluster, and many of you may already be aware of your Starseed origins, though you may be confused about what that means right now. You have a deep desire to help the Earth and its inhabitants, and you want to find a way to make your life count for something meaningful. If this mission resonates with you, it is time to start thinking of ways to become more involved in humanitarian efforts and connect with others who are also seeking a greater purpose. Getting involved in new-age and spiritual communities is a great place to start.

Chapter 6: Sirian Starseeds

Sirius is a star in the Canis Major constellation and the brightest one in the night sky. It's also one of the closest stars to us, which is why scientists have heavily studied it. It is an ancient constellation representing a dog or hunting dog, particularly a large scent hound kept by royalty because of its speed and agility. Since the beginning of time, it has been a significant star. It was valuable to navigators who used it to measure distances in the night sky because it tended to brighten and then fade, allowing mariners to accurately fix their location. When making long journeys and voyages by sea, having a reference point to guide you on your path is always helpful.

The name Sirius comes from the Greek word *"seirios,"* which means scorching or fiery. It's a binary star system, meaning it has two stars: Sirius A and Sirius B. Sirius A is the brighter of the two, with Sirius B orbiting it. Ancient peoples believed that Sirius was a house or home for little dog-like beings, and many Native American tribes have stories about them. They knew that Sirius was a very important part of their existence because it could always be seen in the sky, and its movement helped them tell time, seasons, and even the status of their hunts. It also signified that life was possible on other worlds, specifically, that a star or planet might have life on it.

The origin of the Sirian Starseeds, known as Sirius.
NASA, ESA and G. Bacon (STScI), Public domain, via Wikimedia Commons:
https://commons.wikimedia.org/wiki/File:Sirius_A_and_B_artwork.jpg

Sirian Starseeds

Sirian Starseeds have been coming to the planet Earth for a long time. These beings are often travelers, explorers, and math, science, and technology experts. They have a unique commitment to the advancement of knowledge and space exploration. They have dedicated their lives to truth, spiritual growth, and protecting life. They come to Earth as scientists, astronauts, inventors, philosophers, and spiritual teachers. They are patient, quiet, and love to read. They're free spirits who have a great sense of humor and like to joke around. They are also long-lived, highly intelligent, energetic, yet peaceful beings. Sirians are known for their contributions to the worlds of science, technology, and medicine. They discover cures, inventions, and vaccines for devastating diseases that have ravaged humankind in the past.

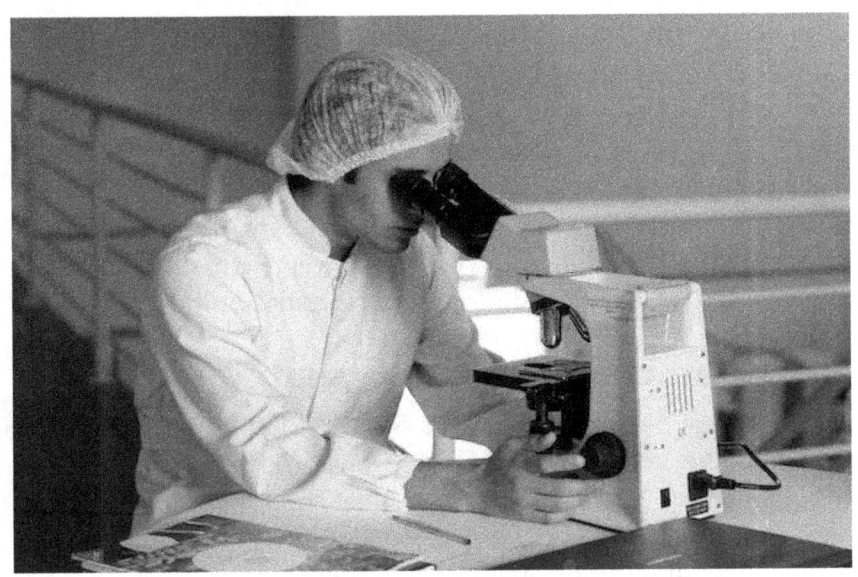

Sirian Starseeds love to benefit our Earth in any way they can.
https://www.pexels.com/photo/adult-biology-chemical-chemist-356040/

Sirians are attracted to people of all races and cultures. They tend to marry outside their race or nationality as they feel a strong sense of curiosity about other cultures and experiences. They also have a universal perspective on life, showing great respect for other races, cultures, and ethnicities. They're open and accepting of all people and value diversity.

These Starseeds typically have a highly developed spirituality and are conscious of their connection to the Earth. They respect nature and maintain a healthy balance between themselves and the world around them. They work diligently to maintain harmony between their surroundings, the environment, and other races. *They are such kind souls*; they are always willing to help others in need, making them natural caregivers. They feel a strong sense of compassion for others and want to heal the world. However, they should be careful about getting involved in everyone else's problems because they could end up neglecting themselves in the process.

Sirian Starseeds are fantastic therapists, teachers, and mentors for children. They're very thoughtful and insightful, and they love to be around children because they're so easy to connect with. These Starseeds can also be very intuitive and can be drawn to careers in the metaphysical or psychic fields. Known for their impeccable control over their emotions, they can make rational decisions when facing difficult situations. They are also highly empathetic and possess an in-depth knowledge of people's intentions, allowing them to predict outcomes and determine if others are being honest with them.

Their creativity and logic are legendary, making them good at solving problems and organizing events. However, they have a temper that makes them take everything personally. So, when something goes wrong, they assume it's their fault and turn their frustration inward.

Characteristics of a Sirian Starseed

1. **Great Sense of Humor**: Sirians love to joke around and make people laugh. They're witty and funny, and they enjoy playing practical jokes on their friends. They love to tell stories and have a great memory for humorous tales, which they don't mind sharing with others.
2. **Deep Thinker**: Sirians are quite analytical and enjoy discussing philosophical or metaphysical ideas with others. They can calm themselves by sitting in silent meditation, allowing their minds to drift away from stress-inducing situations.
3. **High IQ and Discipline:** Sirians love to work hard and stay focused, which makes them excellent students. They are also naturally organized and have a good head for math and science. They excel at problem-solving and logic and are always willing to learn new things.
4. **Strong Intuition:** Sirians have an innate sense of knowing what's happening around them and understand why people act in certain ways. This helps them get involved in the lives of others very easily, as they can relate to others on a deep level.
5. **Good Listeners:** Sirians don't always like to talk because they prefer to listen to others. They are very understanding and try not to judge people. This makes them great listeners, which others open up to quite easily.
6. **Love of Nature:** Sirians are passionate about the environment and try their best to do their part in preserving it. They respect nature and understand its importance in their lives.

7. **Laid-Back:** Sirians don't like to get stressed out or upset over things that they can't control. They tend to make compromises so everyone can enjoy the same level of happiness.
8. **Original Thinker:** Sirians have a good mind for problem-solving and are good at developing new ideas. This makes them extremely creative and innovative in whatever field they find themselves in.
9. **Natural Parent:** Sirians love kids; there's no other way to put it. They have a lot of patience to deal with them and are happy to help out friends with children.

Sirius and the Dogon Tribe

The Dogon Tribe is a group of indigenous people who live in Mali, in Western Africa; they are believed to be the ancestors of the Berbers. The Sirians visited them thousands of years ago, teaching them about astronomy, star worship, and reincarnation. The tribe identified Sirius as the home of beings, or star people, as they called them, who traveled across space in a blue lightship. These wise teachers gave them advanced knowledge of math, science, and medicine. They were responsible for creating the tribe's artwork, carvings, and statues. These star people even helped them build a massive, multistory structure called the granary. It was built on a large scale and was the only one of its kind in the entire region. They were also responsible for creating the tribe's hieroglyphic writings to store their advanced knowledge and wisdom.

Sirius and the Egyptians

Egyptian mythology had many connections to Sirius, and it was often referred to as Sothis. Not much is known about their early connection with the star, but it's suspected that they may have named the star after one of their gods. This would make sense, considering they were spiritual and deeply connected to their beliefs. It's also believed that Sirius may have been an important part of their culture because so many of their symbols are connected to it, including the eye, which represented divinity. They also considered the star a calendar and used it to guide them through the yearly life cycle and seasons. Sirius must have been especially crucial to their religion because the Egyptians claimed it was a portal connecting them to other worlds.

A Message to Sirian Starseeds

Dear Sirian, Starseed, you are called "Sun-seed" because you are the bearers of light and truth and are crucial to humanity as the Aquarius age begins. You contain the wisdom of all ages, and the bloodline from which you have come is significant. The akashic record is stored in the soul, and the physical form is the manifestation of the akashic record. This is why your work as a Starseed depends so much on your bloodline. Investigate your human ancestors to better understand the role you are to play in enhancing this particular bloodline. You are here to upgrade it and to increase spiritual awareness throughout the entire human race.

Your magnetic energy naturally inspires and uplifts others. You are here to guide people toward a higher truth and assist them in reconnecting with their true selves. Your dedication to spiritual work and developing your personal relationships is a priority for you. You are here on Earth to create harmony by bringing people together and creating unique solutions to problems.

You are a direct descendant of the Sirian race, which came to Terra approximately 250,000 years ago, along with the Lyrans. Although there have been many conflicts in this sector of the galaxy and in your own personal lives, you are here to help others resolve emotional and physical imbalances. Your destiny is to assist in the healing process as people awaken to their true spiritual heritage. Your ability to accurately read people and situations is what gives you your magic. Although you may possess many other spiritual gifts, this one stands out.

You are the Sirian Starseed. You are the one who struggles against your own personal limitations. You carry within you the gifts of your ancestors. Deep within you sleeps a mystical power that is awakening in this time of turmoil and chaos, a power that is waiting for the right time to be used to help humanity. Your path has been difficult, but it has led you to where you are today. Yours is the mission of making all things possible. This is your gift and your destiny.

Chapter 7: Lyran Starseeds

Lyra is a constellation of six officially named stars in the Northern celestial hemisphere. It's the smallest of all 88 constellations, but it's packed with interesting features and curious objects. Lyra is dominated by the bluish star Vega, one of the brightest stars in the night sky, with a magnitude of 0.03. Vega is also known for its fast rotation, which causes it to bulge at the equator and flatten at the poles. This unique feature has made it a popular subject of study for astronomers.

Aside from Vega, Lyra also contains several notable deep-sky objects, including the Ring Nebula, a planetary nebula formed when a star similar to our Sun ran out of fuel and shed its outer layers. Another interesting object in Lyra is the Beta Lyrae binary star system, which contains two stars so close together that they appear as one star to the naked eye. The two stars are so close that they revolve around a common center of mass, making them both orbit in the same plane and causing the pair to create a beautiful double image in binoculars. The Double-Double is another double star in Lyra that is visible in binoculars. It lies on the edge of the constellation, and the two stars take about 23 years to revolve around their common center of mass. The two stars are also only one magnitude apart, making them difficult to see together with the naked eye.

Lyran Starseeds are known for their great wisdom and psychic abilities.
https://www.pexels.com/photo/hands-over-fortune-telling-crystal-ball-7179804/

Lyra has been recognized by many cultures throughout history, including the Greeks, who associated it with the mythological figure Orpheus. In Chinese astronomy, Lyra is part of a larger constellation known as the Celestial Bird, and the image of a lyre, a harp-shaped instrument, was once used in the earliest Chinese star maps. Lyra may be small in size, but it's certainly not lacking in intrigue or significance. Its unique features and rich history make it an important area of study for astronomers and spiritualists alike.

Lyran Starseeds

The Lyran Starseeds, highly intelligent, evolved beings from Vega, the brightest planet in the Lyra constellation, are known as the original keepers of ancient knowledge and wisdom. They possess a deep understanding of the universe and its mysteries and are said to have played a key role in the development of human civilization on Earth. The Lyrans are believed to be one of the most ancient Starseed groups, with their origins dating back billions of years. The ancient Lyran civilization is compared to Earth's prehistoric "Romans" or "Egyptians" in the galaxy, and it is unlikely that first-generation Lyrans still exist.

The Lyrans are known throughout the galaxy for their presence in our solar system, and it is said that they first arrived on Earth approximately 4.3 billion years ago. They interacted with some of our earliest civilizations to influence their development here on Earth and appeared as "gods" to those early civilizations, helping teach them about the natural sciences and mystical arts, including astronomy, astrology, alchemy, and so on.

The Lyrans are described as spiritually advanced yet intellectually grounded beings who serve as a support system for other Starseeds. Their focus is on the expansion of consciousness and knowledge, particularly spiritual knowledge and wisdom that's beyond the grasp of normal human consciousness.

The Lyrans work with other Starseeds and assist them as they evolve their consciousness, imparting their wisdom and guidance where they are needed most. The Lyrans are said to have especially interacted with the Lemurians, considered to be humankind's early ancestors on Earth. These ancient beings are also closely tied to the Vegan Starseeds, who some believe to be their offspring.

Unlike other Starseeds, which are often associated with one particular star in a constellation, the Lyrans have their origins among the planets and stars of the Lyra constellation. This means that most Lyran Starseeds don't have a home planet to call their own. Instead, they form communities or nomadic groups to live on different planets while traveling back and forth between them and Vega.

Lyran Starseeds are said to possess high levels of psychic and creative abilities, which are believed to be amplified while traveling and living among other Starseed groups. They are also believed to have certain powers allowing them to heal their emotional and physical bodies. With this ability, they can work with a person's chakras, bringing them back into alignment by opening up blocked energy centers and facilitating energy flow through them.

Characteristics of a Lyran Starseed

Lyran Starseeds have several qualities that make them stand out from other Starseeds. The following are some of the traits that these Starseeds may experience or display throughout their lives:

- **You Feel Like an Old Soul:** Lyran Starseeds often have a deep sense of wisdom and understanding beyond their years. You may feel like you have been on this earth for a long time, even if you are relatively young. This is because Lyrans have a strong connection to their past lives and ancestral lineage, which gives them a sense of grounding and stability in this lifetime.

- **You Love Adventure:** You have a great sense of adventure that can take you to interesting places. You really love the thrill of discovery and enjoy going to new and exotic places.

- **You Are an Enthusiastic Traveler:** You love traveling in other realms just as much as you enjoy exploring the physical world, so you are drawn to astral projection, lucid dreaming, and out-of-body experiences. These activities allow you to broaden your perspective and see things from different points of view. By observing these alternative realities through different lenses, you can learn a lot about yourself and our world.

- **You Are Drawn to History and Historical Events:** You are also fascinated by ancient knowledge from civilizations throughout the ages. You want to explore the mysteries and secrets of the past to learn how to better understand the present and future.

- **You Tend to Go with the Flow of Life:** Lyran Starseeds have a deep sense of trust in the universe and its plan for them. They don't resist change or try to control outcomes but instead allow life to unfold naturally. This doesn't mean they're passive or lack ambition, but rather that they're open to new experiences and opportunities that come their way.

- **You Easily Manifest Your Reality:** Lyran Starseeds possess a powerful ability to effortlessly manifest their desires. They understand that their thoughts and emotions directly impact their reality and use this knowledge to create the life they want. They don't struggle or fight to make things happen but instead trust that the universe will bring them what they need at the right time.

- **You Are Not the Most Patient:** While Lyran Starseeds have a strong sense of trust in the universe, they can sometimes struggle with patience. They have a deep desire to see their dreams come to fruition quickly and may become frustrated when things don't happen as fast as they would like. However, they understand that everything happens in divine timing and that their impatience can actually block the flow of abundance. As such, they work on cultivating patience and surrendering to the natural flow of life.

- **You Value Authenticity:** Lyran Starseeds place a high value on authenticity and genuineness. They believe being true to oneself is essential for personal growth and spiritual evolution. They are not interested in putting on a façade or pretending to be someone they are not, as they know that this only hinders their progress. Instead, they strive to be honest and transparent in all their interactions with themselves and others. This commitment to authenticity allows them to form deep and meaningful connections with those around them and the universe itself.

- **You Are Fascinated by the Magical Arts:** You are endlessly curious about the intricate rituals, the ancient symbols, and the mystical energies surrounding us. You spend countless hours studying and practicing various forms of divination, from tarot readings to crystal scrying. Your intuition is finely tuned, and you trust your inner guidance to lead you on your spiritual path. You seek out like-minded individuals who share your passion for the occult, and together, you explore the mysteries of the universe. You have gained a deeper understanding of yourself and the world around you through dedication to the magical arts. You know there is much more to life than meets the eye, and you constantly seek new ways to connect with the divine. Your journey is one of self-discovery and enlightenment, and you embrace it with open arms.

Myth and Lore

The story of the Lyra constellation begins with the Greek mythological figure of Orpheus. Orpheus was the son of Apollo, the god of music and prophecy, and Calliope, one of the Muses. He was a skilled musician and poet who played songs that could move even rocks to tears. He had a wife named Eurydice, who died from a snake bite, and in an act of grief, he ventured into the underworld to bring her back to life. Hoping that music would soothe Hades' heart, Orpheus played such sad songs that Hades wept for him. Touched by Orpheus' music, Hades allowed Eurydice to return to the land of the living with one condition—Orpheus could not look back at her until they had left the underworld.

However, when he finally reached the surface and opened his eyes, he realized that she wasn't behind him. In his haste to get her, he disobeyed the rule of Hades and looked back before she reached safety. As a result, Eurydice disappeared back into the underworld forever.

Orpheus was devastated and spent the rest of his life mourning her loss. He wandered the earth, playing mournful tunes on his lyre, hoping to find solace in his music. His songs were so sorrowful that even the animals and trees would weep when they heard him play. Eventually, his grief became too much to bear, and he decided to join Eurydice in the underworld. He descended into Hades' realm again, but this time he was not allowed to leave. His tragic story moved the gods, and they placed his lyre in the sky as a constellation so that his music could continue to be heard for eternity. And so, Orpheus' legacy lived on through his music, a testament to the power of love and the pain of loss.

A Message for the Lyran Starseed

Dear Lyran Starseed, you are not alone in this universe. Your soul comes from the Lyra constellation, a place of great spiritual power and wisdom. You have been sent to Earth to share your unique gifts and help raise the collective consciousness of humanity. Your mission is not easy, but it is filled with purpose and meaning.

Like Orpheus, you have a special connection to music and the arts. Your creative talents are a powerful tool for healing and transformation. Use them wisely and with intention, for they can touch people's hearts in ways that words cannot. But remember, your journey on Earth is not without its challenges. The pain of loss may be something you are familiar with, but it can also teach you great lessons about the nature of love and the human experience.

As you navigate this life, know that your spirit guides and higher self are always with you, offering guidance and support along the way. They have watched over you since the beginning of time and will continue to offer you strength and guidance in your life's journey.

Don't be afraid to reach out for help when you need it, for many people can help you on your path. And know that the journey is not over until it is complete. Follow your spirit and keep moving forward, for this is how you'll find your way home again, to the stars from whence you came.

Chapter 8: Orion Starseeds

Orion is a wonderful constellation for stargazers and people who just want to bask in the glory of nature's wonderment. The physical body of this constellation is visible from anywhere on Earth (except Antarctica), so it's easy to find with some simple calculations and by looking through a telescope or binoculars. Three stars in this constellation form a bright and easily recognizable belt. Alnitak is the highest of the three but not the brightest. Alnilam is slightly lower and is a supergiant star, the brightest in the belt. It has about 374,000 times the Sun's luminosity and is 1,300 light years away from Earth. Mintaka is on a lower level than Alnilam and is actually a binary star system, which means that there is a smaller companion star orbiting it. This celestial pattern was first observed by the ancient Greeks and was said to represent a hunter's belt.

Orion Starseeds have guided humanity through evolutionary stages and still are.
https://www.pexels.com/photo/concentrated-young-multiethnic-friends-with-map-in-railway-station-6140458/

On the other hand, Orion's three belt stars aren't the only bright stars in the constellation. There are actually a total of seven bright stars in Orion: Alnitak, Alnilam, Mintaka, Betelgeuse (which is Orion's right shoulder), Bellatrix (his left shoulder), Saiph (his right knee), and Rigel (his foot). The brightest of these stars is Rigel, a blue-white supergiant and the 8th brightest star in the night sky.

Several deep-sky objects in Orion may also interest stargazers and amateur astronomers. The Great Orion Nebula is one of the brightest diffuse nebulae in the sky. It's so bright that it can be seen with the naked eye from a dark site without binoculars or a telescope. It is believed to be an interstellar cloud of gas and dust, a wonderful home to many new stars being born and many old stars dying.

Orion Starseeds

The Orion Starseeds are a race of benevolent explorers who have been guiding Earth's evolution for millennia. They represent an advanced society that has mastered space travel and other galactic technologies. Choosing to become the caretakers of our planet, they have been with us during our most important evolutionary stages. The last ice age is a good example. They were present behind the scenes, helping to facilitate our species' survival by providing us with technology and watching for the most advantageous times to influence particular events.

It has been speculated that beings from Orion created Atlantis and Lemuria, during which time they taught us how to use crystals and heal ourselves. They were also involved in mankind's move from Lemuria to Atlantis and the beginning of this civilization. They then helped us with the move from Atlantis to Egypt, where they taught us hieroglyphics, mathematics, and advanced agriculture.

Over many thousands of years, the Orions have guided us through times of great change. They are among the few star races with an affinity with Earth, which resonates with their personal experiences here. It's been said that they have spent thousands of years in various incarnations on Earth, from giants to humans, and their influence is still present in many places on Earth today through their artifacts buried in the soil or secret chambers hidden deep beneath oceans and ancient mountains.

Orion Starseeds are known for their compassion, generosity, and love of human beings. They are very aware of the value of life and work hard to keep life-giving systems healthy. They also have an inherent need to study humanity as a species to better understand our nature and what we need.

They believe in continuous learning and will always seek out opportunities for growth and personal development. They are very much into the whole concept of evolution and will often be found observing other planets through telescopes or other forms of remote sensing. Some can astrally travel through the stars as well as space, which allows them to easily move from planet to planet, star system to star system, or galaxy to galaxy.

Characteristics of an Orion Starseed

- **You Can Be Accurately Described as Curious**: Orion Starseeds are very concerned about education and will always try to learn as much as possible. They are very inquisitive about the nature of the universe and seek to understand how it all works. They always want to know how things evolve from one state to another and why they take a particular path.
- **You Are Extremely Creative**: The Orion Starseeds are extremely capable of coming up with ideas that can help solve problems. They are very good problem solvers and excel at putting things together in a way that never existed before. They have an innovative mind that beautifully combines existing information and skills to create something unique and untested.
- **You Are Vigilant, Attentive, and Insightful**: The Orion Starseeds are always aware of their surroundings and will not allow anything to happen without their knowledge or approval. They will be the first to notice anything that is out of the ordinary and are always on the verge of discovering, ready to make sense of new things they encounter. They try to anticipate what is going to happen and have a plan for how to act accordingly.
- **You Take Your Duties Very Seriously:** This is one of the most important characteristics found in Orion Starseeds. They know what is right and what is wrong and won't allow themselves to get caught up in things that cause harm to others or themselves. They are very conscious of their destiny and will do everything possible to ensure their own well-being and that of other entities within their sphere of influence.

- **You Are Compassionate**: Orion Starseeds place a lot of importance on human life and will always try to help those in need. They would go out of their way to save someone from a burning building or stop a violent attack. They believe in supporting the less fortunate whenever possible and enjoy helping others when they can without needing to receive anything in return.

- **You Are Curious about Spirituality:** Orion Starseeds will always pursue spiritual enlightenment and answers to the mysteries of life. They want to understand their own existence and how they fit into the bigger picture. They will never be satisfied unless they know how everything fits together and why certain things happen.

- **You Love a Good Challenge:** Orion Starseeds enjoy being challenged. When they are presented with a situation that seems daunting to everyone else, they will jump on it. It allows them to sharpen their skills and apply their intelligence in ways that matter to them. They don't like the feeling of defeat and will apply whatever pressure it takes to ensure the desired outcome. They are natural-born athletes, explorers, and pioneers because they love the thrill of conquering a difficult task or goal. Once they have reached a certain milestone, they are not the type to just bask in that achievement; they want more.

- **You Are a Natural Leader:** Orion Starseeds can be found leading groups of people and have a natural way of inspiring those with whom they work alongside. They are very good at giving directions and finding ways to make them both efficient and creative at the same time. You'll find them at the frontlines, where everyone can see them, and they will give commands that the rest of the crowd will follow without question. They enjoy being in charge and will always take on a leadership role whenever possible.

- **You Are Opinionated:** Orion Starseeds have a strong sense of self and always follow their own intuition. They are not the type to shy away from raising their voice to make an important point or stand up for what they believe is right. They are very determined to get others to see the world as they do, and this can be very challenging for them when faced with people who oppose their belief system.

Myth and Lore

The earliest account of this tale describes Orion as the child of the god Poseidon and Euryale, princess of King Minos of Crete. One day, he set out determined to reach the island of Chios, and he succeeded because of his father, who gave him the ability to walk on water. Drunk out of his mind, he attempted to seduce Merope, the local king's daughter; as punishment, he was blinded and thrown off the island by King Oenopion. Blind Orion quickly made his way to Lemnos, the location of the forge that belonged to the god Hephaestus, and with the aid of the fire god, Orion made it to the East, where the sun god Helios healed his blindness.

With his sight restored, Orion continued his travels, eventually returning to Crete, where he met Princess Artemis. The two quickly fell in love and became inseparable. Together, they hunted and roamed the countryside, with Orion's skills as a hunter impressing even the goddess of the hunt herself. However, their happiness was short-lived as Apollo, Artemis' twin brother, became jealous of their relationship and tricked Artemis into killing Orion. Devastated by her actions, Artemis pleaded with Zeus to place Orion among the stars as a constellation. There, he could be forever remembered as the greatest hunter that ever lived.

A Message for the Orion Starseed

Dear Orion Starseed, it's time for you to open your eyes and see the world for what it truly is. Life has been a series of tests, but now you are ready to enter a whole new world that hasn't even begun to be explored yet by the rest of humanity. You have been chosen to face this huge task as a leader on behalf of your community. You were selected because you have courage and spiritual strength. It is your time to shine because everyone is waiting for you to step up and bring them into this brave new world you envisioned.

The time of ruling one another is at an end. It's time to create a society where spirituality is valued, and those who are the leaders on all levels of the hierarchy are in their positions because of their character and not because of their wealth or good looks. It's time for everyone to know the truth about how we got here and what our purpose really is as a species. You'll help humanity realize all these things, but you'll have to be patient and let things progress at the pace that they need to. It's been a long time coming, and things will happen as soon as they are ready. So, keep your head up and trust that the universe is on your side.

Chapter 9: Arcturian Starseeds

Arcturus is a red giant star located in the constellation of Boötes. It is one of the brightest stars in the night sky and is easily visible to the naked eye. It is around 37 light-years from Earth and is the brightest star in its constellation. The star's surface temperature is around 4,300 Kelvin, giving it its distinctive orange-red color, and it has a diameter approximately 25 times larger than that of our sun.

Despite being an old star, Arcturus still shines brightly due to its size and high luminosity. It is estimated to be around 7 billion years old, meaning it has already exhausted most of its hydrogen fuel and will eventually evolve into a white dwarf star. Despite being well-known as the brightest star in its constellation, another interesting fact about this red giant is that it is believed to be the home star of the Arcturian race, which includes many humanoid extraterrestrials.

The home star of the Arcturian Starseeds. S
Roberto Mura, CC BY-SA 4.0 <https://creativecommons.org/licenses/by-sa/4.0>, via Wikimedia Commons: https://commons.wikimedia.org/wiki/File:Arcturus_DSS.png

Arcturian Starseeds

Arcturian Starseeds have incarnated on Earth from the Arcturus star system. In most cases, they don't realize they come from Arcturus until much later in life. They are often strongly interested in space, science, philosophy, metaphysics, and esoteric fields. They also have an interest in exploring the unknown, which could be how they got here in the first place over 120,000 years ago.

Arcturian Starseeds often feel like they don't belong on Earth and like they are only here for a reason. An Arcturian Starseed can experience bouts of depression or fatigue due to the extreme contrast between how they feel on the inside and how they appear to be on the outside. Some may feel trapped in their physical bodies and the third dimension, but when they awaken to their true nature, they will be able to see that this was a vehicle for their consciousness to explore and develop in.

According to Edgar Cayce, the existence of Arcturians is thought to take place in a dimension of clarity beyond human comprehension. Humans would find their planet's purity and clarity to be very energizing, and upon first contact with them, one would feel a personal purification. With the Arcturians, there would no longer be any need for the extra baggage we have in this third-dimensional world, and this world would be able to heal from its current state of disrepair.

Arcturians don't worry about things like physical survival, safety, retirement, pensions, or even simple forms of labor. These topics are outside of their purview. Instead, they give their time and energy to the spiritual life but do not mistake this for a life without pleasure. They also have relationships and enjoy music. They work as well, but not at the level of squalor required by our culture and society. Their work better fits their personal preferences and spiritual journeys.

Arcturians are also extremely peaceful people. They haven't fought in battle in a very long time. Yes, they are capable of appearing in the third dimension, and yes, they can defend themselves if need be, but they typically aren't involved in anything that even remotely resembles a conflict. It is said that they can instantly dematerialize if there is a problem. Any projectile that comes their way would simply pass through them without harming them. This is a skill that some other extraterrestrial civilizations have mastered.

Arcturians also experience the death of their form on Arcturus, but they do so in a very different way because it is only seen as a temporary phase of their existence, not as the end. When they incarnate on Earth, they'd rather spend their time enjoying the physical world and using it as a way to experience more diversity and clarity of consciousness. The idea of aging would be looked upon with a sense of humor. We can learn something from this and embrace the present because it is an opportunity to use the here and now as an arena for experiencing who we are.

Another thing of note is that Arcturians haven't been directly involved in the genetic or evolutionary changes that have occurred in human DNA. The Sirians and Pleiadians were left to handle those matters. Arcturians primarily served as supervisors or teachers, and now they are here to assist us in completing our cycle so that we can enter the stargate and ascend to the fifth dimension.

Characteristics of an Arcturian Starseed

- **You Are Highly Organized:** You like to be precise with time and life events. You are meticulous with your work schedule and appointments.
- **You Are Mostly Interested in Science and Technology:** You enjoy exploring the mysteries of life through technology, scientific experiments, space travel, computers, medicine, and alternative healing techniques. There is a tendency to be an over thinker, and you want to understand everything in depth.
- **You Are Very Mysterious:** Getting to know you is hard because you keep your personal life private. You are a solid friend and family member but are cautious when disclosing information about yourself. It is rare for you to get close to someone or open up too quickly.
- **You Love Your Space:** While you enjoy socializing with close friends and family, you often need alone time to recharge your batteries. You enjoy sitting by yourself and watching the stars. It's not uncommon for you to have a nagging feeling that you don't really belong here on Earth. It could be the crowds, cities, or intense environments.
- **You Have a Knack for Public Speaking:** You are good at giving speeches and expressing your ideas. You know how to get

people to listen to you when you are passionate about a subject.

- **You Value Logic:** You tend to use your mind more than your heart when dealing with problems and making decisions. You can analyze situations objectively and come up with practical solutions. This will serve you well in business but not so well in relationships.
- **You Love Creating:** Despite your logical nature, you also have a creative side. You enjoy writing, drawing, or playing music in your spare time. It's one of the few ways you express yourself.
- **You Are Very Intuitive:** You feel that there is a greater truth in the universe that cannot be unraveled by reason alone. Your intuition is a great guide for you, but it can also cause you to feel lonely or isolated from other people at times because it is not something everyone understands or comprehends.
- **You Have an Incredible Eye for Detail:** You can easily become bored or frustrated if things don't have a certain degree of precision. You have a passion for accuracy and ensure everything is in its proper place, just like it should be. It's one reason you don't like to be around those who are not as organized and precise.

Myth and Lore

At least two Greek myths feature Arcturus. The first connects Arcas and Callisto's constellations, Boötes and Ursa Major. In this tale, Hera, the wife of Zeus, changed Callisto into a bear after learning of her husband's adultery. Callisto wandered the woods for a while before she ran into her grown-up son, Arcas. Arcas pulled his spear out of fear for the large bear in front of him. Zeus, however, stepped in right away to avert a catastrophe. Callisto and Arcas were taken up into the heavens by a whirlwind; Arcas was turned into Boötes, and Callisto became Ursa Major.

Arcturus is also linked to the legend of Icarius in another myth. Icarius, an Athenaean, received the gift of wine as a token of appreciation from the god Dionysus. He proceeded to give the wine to some shepherds he encountered, and they became drunk. Thinking Icarus had poisoned them, they killed him and left his body in the bushes. Erigone, Icarius' daughter, and Maera, her dog, soon came upon his body, and they were so distraught that they committed suicide.

Dionysus decided to punish the city of Athens with a plague because he was so furious. The plague finally ended after the Athenians instituted rituals to remember Icarius and Erigone. Icarius, Erigone, and Maera were transformed by Dionysus into the constellations Boötes, Virgo, and the star Procyon (Maera).

A Message for the Arcturian Starseed

Dear Arcturian Starseed, know that your unique perspective on the world is truly a gift. Your ability to see things precisely and clearly is a rare talent that should be celebrated. However, I also understand that this can sometimes make you feel isolated or misunderstood by others who may not share your level of awareness. You must remember that while your perception may differ, it doesn't make it any less valid or valuable. Embrace your individuality and continue to use your keen eye for detail to make positive changes in the world around you. But don't forget to stay open to new ideas and experiences. You must be willing to understand why people do the things they do if you hope to form positive relationships with them. You must learn to be flexible if you want to adapt to different circumstances as they arise.

You are here to do great things, and nothing will stand in your way. Paradoxically, the very thing you are most gifted at doing is also what will trip you up the most. Be careful that your critical eye does not become so focused on the things that need to be improved that it causes you to miss seeing the beauty in what already exists.

Don't let other people's reactions prevent you from doing what makes your heart happy or allowing yourself the freedom of experimentation. Your awareness is a gift that needs to be treated with respect and dignity. You must also learn to balance your need for personal space with your desire for close relationships. You already have a strong support network in place, and all you need to do is trust yourself enough to allow them into your life. Change is scary sometimes, but that's what makes it so exhilarating.

Chapter 10: Vega Starseeds

Vega is a star in the Lyra constellation that is known for its brightness and beauty. It is the fifth-brightest star in the sky and can be seen from almost anywhere on Earth. It is also a relatively young star, estimated to be only about 455 million years old. It has a mass roughly 2.1 times that of the sun and a radius about 2.7 times larger. Vega's temperature is also much hotter than the sun, with a surface temperature of around 9,600 Kelvin.

One of the most interesting things about Vega is its rapid rotation, which causes it to bulge at the equator and flatten at the poles. This phenomenon is known as oblateness and is a result of the centrifugal force generated by Vega's fast spin. In addition to that, Vega is classified as a blue-white star, meaning that it emits most of its light in the blue and ultraviolet parts of the spectrum, making it one of the brightest stars in the sky and an important target for astronomers studying stellar evolution.

In recent years, Vega has been found to have a debris disk—a ring of dust and debris orbiting around it—which could indicate collisions between asteroids or comets or the presence of exoplanets. The study of Vega's debris disk has provided valuable insights into the formation and evolution of planetary systems, as it is believed that such disks are the birthplace of planets. In fact, the presence of a debris disk around Vega suggests that there may be planets orbiting the star, although none have been detected yet, at least not scientifically. Scientists continue to study Vega and its surrounding environment to better understand the processes that shape our universe. As technology advances and new discoveries are made, we can expect to learn more about this fascinating star and its mysteries.

The Vega star, where the Vega Starseeds came from.
Morigan221, CC BY-SA 3.0 <https://creativecommons.org/licenses/by-sa/3.0>, via Wikimedia Commons: https://commons.wikimedia.org/wiki/File:Vega_-_star_in_Lyra.png

Vega Starseeds

The brightest star system in the constellation of Lyra, Vega, is the origin of the alien species known as the Vega Starseed. They are also referred to as Vegans, and no, this has zero to do with the diet. Vegans came from Lyra so that they could colonize and rule Sirius, the dog star. They are said to be descendants of the oldest known humanoid species and are, without a doubt, the most advanced in this galaxy. Of course, they can also reincarnate on Earth, where they typically assume a humanoid form with gorgeous dark skin and raven hair. Some also come in subtle copper undertones, enhancing their ethereal beauty. Still, on their home planet, their skin is said to have a bluish tint.

The Vega Starseed has many characteristics of an enlightened being, but none is more important than loving unconditionally. This means that their love extends to all sentient beings, even those who do not meet their standards for behavior. When it comes to relationships, they are both empathetic and extremely seductive. They have huge hearts and are always willing to listen to the needs of others, but they will never allow themselves to be taken advantage of. Though they are extremely generous with their love and support, they do not make it a habit of allowing themselves to be used. If anyone ever tries to manipulate them into giving more than what is reasonable, they will show that person the door—no exceptions.

Vegans' amount of love has no limit.
https://www.pexels.com/photo/studio-shot-of-mother-and-daughter-hugging-17049338/

Many Vegans are kind, but that is not always the case. They are also known to be completely ruthless and unforgiving if anyone should betray them or cross them in any way. They are not above doing whatever it takes to exact revenge, and they will not think twice about doing so if warranted. These people are far more advanced than humans could ever imagine, and because of their exceptional talent and creativity, they have been able to settle on or colonize several planets in our galaxy. Regardless, they are a friendly species because they have empathy and are old souls who are extremely conscious of the universe's interconnectedness.

Characteristics of a Vega Starseed

- **Inconsistent Yet Creative:** They are extremely creative and intelligent but also very unpredictable. They often switch between having unconventional beliefs one day and acting far more conventionally the next.

- **Like to Live in Exotic Places:** Many Vega Starseeds go out of their way to visit different countries in search of that one place where they can feel at home. They are almost addicted to moving around and enjoy traveling to remote locations with breathtaking scenery.

- **Can Be Very Officious:** If you are working with a Vega Starseed, do not forget that they have their own ideas of what is acceptable and what is not. You may think you can boss them around, but your chances of success are slim. Their confidence in who they are will not allow them to be pressured into doing something just because someone else thinks it should be done a certain way.

- **Always Seeking to Learn More:** Vega Starseeds are always seeking to gather more information about themselves and the world around them. They keep an open mind and like to discuss and debate various ideas that they come across.

- **The Center of Attention:** Usually, these individuals are excellent conversationalists, which means that they can talk just about anyone into anything. This is a natural gift for them, but it also comes in handy when they try to tell you why you should do what they want you to do.

- **Are Not Afraid to Look into the Future:** Though many humans have this ability, Vega Starseeds are especially good at it because they have a natural knack for intuition. They love working with channels, tarot cards, and other forms of mediumship because it allows them to tap into their abilities even further.

- **Not Afraid to Let You Know What They Are Thinking:** Vega Starseeds are open about their feelings, and if you have them as a friend, they will be honest enough to tell you exactly what they think of you. This is both a blessing and a curse because they will not hesitate to tell you about it when things go wrong in the relationship.

- **Can Be Ruthless:** When betrayed, Vega Starseeds are known to easily turn on their former friends and close associates. They tend to cut people off without a second thought – and never look back.
- **Fiercely Loyal:** Vega Starseeds are protective of the ones they love and will go to great lengths to protect them from the harshness of this world. This can sometimes manifest as obsession, so they must learn to set healthy boundaries with their loved ones.

Myth and Lore

According to legend, Vega, a goddess of the heavens, and Altair, a human, were once lovers. Vega, the princess of the skies, felt very alone and isolated as she flew through the heavens. One day, she approached a handsome man she had seen sitting beneath a large tree to listen to the music he was playing on his flute. He was delighted and surprised to see her, and he immediately fell in love with her. In the days that followed, she paid him a visit every day because she had fallen in love with the Earthly cow herder. She promised that no matter what happened, they would be in the Heavens one day together.

In some versions of the story, her mother is the one who learns about the forbidden romance. It's her father in others. However, the outcome is the same: they drag Vega away and forbid her from seeing this mortal. A cruel turn of events sees the fulfillment of her promise, and the two lovers are placed in the skies, though they are far apart and will always be divided by the Heavens. With Vega in the constellation Lyra and Altair in the constellation Aquila, the Great Celestial River, which is the Milky Way, lay between them.

A bridge of magpies is said to form once a year on the seventh day of the seventh month of the traditional Chinese calendar, letting the lovers be together for a single day. However, it's not always feasible to meet. The legend claims that if it rains on this day, the lovers will not be able to see one another and that the rain is actually Vega's tears falling from the heavens.

The story of Vega and Altair gives people hope that, against all odds and despite the extreme distance, people who are connected at heart can still find each other, even if it takes a while. There is always a chance where there is great love.

A Message for the Vega Starseed

Dear Vega Starseed, you have done this a thousand times over in a thousand different lifetimes. You have had many names, but you are always the same person. You are a warrior, a protector, and a guardian of light. Your fierce loyalty is one of your greatest strengths but can also be your downfall if you do not learn to balance it with healthy boundaries. Remember that you cannot save everyone, and sometimes the best thing you can do is let go and trust that they will find their own way.

Your mission on this planet is to bring light and love to those who need it most. You are here to heal the wounds of the past and create a brighter future for all beings. But to do this, you must first heal yourself. Take time to connect with your inner self and listen to the whispers of your soul. Trust your intuition and follow your heart, even when it leads you down an unfamiliar path. You possess many gifts but are only as powerful as you choose to be.

Chapter 11: Maldekian Starseeds

This chapter is about a planet believed to have existed eons ago. The asteroid belt (which includes the dwarf planet Ceres) is thought to have formed as a result of Phaeton (or Maldek), a hypothetical planet that the Titius-Bode law hypothesized may have existed between Mars and Jupiter's orbits. The fictitious planet was named "*Phaeton*" in honor of Phaethon, a character from Greek mythology who attempted unsuccessfully for one day to drive his father's solar chariot before being slain by Zeus.

Phaeton is a fascinating concept that has captured the imagination of scientists and astronomers for centuries. While it remains a hypothetical planet scientifically, the idea of its existence has helped us better understand the formation of our solar system. The asteroid belt we know today is believed to be the remnants of Phaeton, which was destroyed in a catastrophic collision with another celestial body. It is believed that this event may have also contributed to the formation of Jupiter's moons and even Earth. Even though many scientists have disregarded its existence, Phaeton has left an indelible mark on our understanding of the universe and serves as a reminder of the enigmas that still await us in space.

Maldekian Starseeds are mysterious and secretive except with their trusted ones.
https://www.pexels.com/photo/eye-looking-at-the-camera-3712574/

Maldekian Starseeds

All you have read so far is science's version of the story. Let's look at what mediums, spiritualists, and esotericism have to say about it. Trusted channelers have revealed that Phaeton, which was actually called *Maldek*, was run into the ground by invaders. Imagine the world in a thousand years with nuclear war, pollution, and survivors in underground bunkers believing they are safe from harm. This was Maldek at some point in their history. It was once a planet occupied by light beings with infinite wisdom and knowledge. There was even a time when angels used it as a base between incarnations and missions. Maldek was incredibly old, with some saying it existed before the Pleiades. The beings there were incredibly misunderstood but still gave unconditional love.

Their planet was invaded by a different race, which attempted to seize total control of the area, and the Maldekians engaged in a losing battle for survival. They shared the same technology but were too full of love to actually use it against the other group. As a result, Maldek exploded into pieces as the invaders dealt the final blow. While some souls could move onto higher dimensions, Maldek itself ceased to exist. Also breaking into tiny pieces was the consciousness of Maldekians, and according to channeled transmissions, there are many Maldekian souls with fragments of themselves dispersed throughout the cosmos.

That is too much agony to experience, and it's unlikely to go away in a few lifetimes. It travels with them. They tend to feel lost and would like to go home, but they never do because they are aware in the back of their minds that their home has already been lost. As Starseeds, they experience feelings of having a twin or being lost and cut off from the family they were born into. They've never had a sense of community. They have grieving souls and appear to be in pain, but they are never sure why. The source of their suffering is deeper than meets the eye, so they are usually given diagnoses for manic depression and anxiety disorders without any basis in fact.

Maldekian Starseeds typically gravitate toward archeology because they are looking for anything their kind left behind on this planet, as many came here after the catastrophe that befell their home. They would have settled in hot, dry areas like ancient Egypt or Mexico or areas with high altitudes such as the Andes, Alps, Rockies, and Himalayas. They would have been among the first alien populations to thrive on Earth because they were once highly advanced.

Maldekians are very sensitive to materialism, yet they still crave material things like art that is created with care and love. They don't need to read a book because they are inherently wise. They are easily bored here because they are already familiar with everything. They are obstinate and strong-willed and prefer to observe others while remaining inconspicuous. Although they usually try to keep a low profile to avoid missing anything, they are quite sociable. However, they lack relationships and are very untrusting. They don't often get married, but when they do, they mate for life.

They have a crude sense of humor that borders on slapstick, especially when acting extremely silly for amusement. These souls will laugh at anything because laughter, as people say, is the best medicine. It makes them feel better, and it will also make people around them laugh.

Their physical appearance is usually striking. They are beautiful and fascinating but very mysterious at the same time. Maldekian Starseeds always appear very old and wise, with a haunted look in their eyes. Despite their good nature and willingness to go above and beyond for others, they have a darker side. They are well-liked by others but dislike others. Despite being a loner, they appear well-known and friendly around other people. However, only those who share their values can see their true colors because they are secretive and refuse to let others in. They are excellent at lying, not because they are dishonest people but as a coping mechanism that prevents them from telling others what they really think or how they truly feel.

Characteristics of a Maldekian Starseed

- They are sensitive and have a deep longing to feel safe.
- They might appear very wise but have an inquisitive nature that can border on insubordination.
- They could also appear withdrawn and lonely, but they are very sociable with their own kind.
- In stressful situations, they will react violently or verbally aggressively towards those around them because they feel threatened in some way by this person, people, or situation.
- They can be very rebellious, stubborn, or unyielding.
- They could appear to be self-centered and selfish when, in reality, they're just trying to protect themselves from others' criticism, as they are overly sensitive and easily hurt.
- They are drawn to fire and bright light.
- Their lives tend to be uneventful and boring because they are not interested in action or adventure.

Myth and Lore

The child of Helios, the sun god, and Clymene, a mortal, Phaethon resided with his mother due to his father's challenging task. Helios was in charge of driving the Sun's chariot across the Earth during the day, which resulted in the sun rising and setting.

One day, a classmate of Phaethon's made fun of him for saying he was the god's son and stated he didn't believe him. In sorrow, Phaethon requested proof of his paternity from his mother. After reassuring him that he was, in fact, the son of the mighty god Helios, Clymene sent her son to his father's palace to demonstrate his legitimacy.

India was home to his father's palace, where he was meant to begin each day's journey from the East. So Phaethon set out, full of joy and optimism. He told Helios about the humiliation he had to go through due to being accused of being an illegitimate child. He begged Helios to acknowledge him as his son and prove conclusively that he was the son of the Sun god. Deeply moved, Helios firmly confirmed Phaethon's legitimacy and paternity. He even said in front of everyone present that he would happily do his son any favors he requested.

Happy that the great Helios had acknowledged him as his son, Phaethon decided to put his father's love and generosity to the test. The brazen boy requested permission to drive the magnificent Chariot of the Sun for a single day. Concerned about his son's absurd request, Helios tried to persuade him that not even the powerful Zeus, much less a simple mortal, could pilot the Chariot of the Sun. Only the god Helios received that challenging assignment.

Unfortunately, they could not retract or change their minds once the gods committed. However, Helios tried in vain to convince the hurried Phaethon to back off from making his absurd demand. It was one thing to want to pilot the magnificent Chariot of the Sun, but to actually pull it off was more difficult than our naive Phaethon had anticipated.

As soon as he set off, Phaethon realized he had bitten off more than he could chew. The vicious horses began to follow a wild and dangerous course once they grasped the immaturity and inexperience of their young charioteer, and he discovered that he was entirely unable to control them.

The unstoppable Chariot of the Sun began to descend too low, and as it did, it crashed into the planet and unleashed a torrent of calamity, burning the African continent until it was a desert, causing terrible damage to the Nile River, and even turning the Ethiopians black from exposure to the Sun's fire.

Zeus was furious. All this destruction by the insolent boy made him fume. He struck Phaethon with a thunderbolt to prevent anything else, and the dead boy washed into the Eridanus River, subsequently known as the Italian River Po.

A Message for the Maldekian Starseed

Dear Maldekian Starseed, you are a wonderful person whose role in life is to help others. You may feel sad or angry at the world because of things that have happened to you, but don't let that overwhelm you. Your task is to help heal the planet and defeat evil forces wherever they appear. You have always known who you were and what you were meant to do, but now it's time for everyone else to know who you really are.

You'll be called crazy, and many people will attempt to silence your voice of truth, but you'll continue to speak your truth anyway. The people of Maldek are not who they seem to be, but neither are the world's ruling classes. You can see through their facades and deceptive masks when others can't. Your mission is to expose their true intentions and bring justice to those oppressed for far too long.

Your journey will not be easy, but it will be worth it. You'll encounter obstacles and challenges along the way, but you must stay strong and never give up. Remember that you are not alone in this fight; there are others who share your vision and will stand by your side. Together, you can create a better world for future generations. It's time to step into your power and fulfill your destiny as a warrior of light. The universe is waiting for you to make your mark and leave a lasting impact on this planet. So go forth with courage and determination, knowing you have the strength to accomplish anything you set your mind to. Believe in yourself and trust that your actions, no matter how small, can make a difference. The world is waiting for you.

Chapter 12: Avian Starseeds

Those who belong to the Avian race are a class of celestial beings from an entirely different universe, not even another planet or galaxy. These prehistoric life forms were master geneticists and creators who significantly impacted the multiverse's diversity by seeding the universe with various species. This is why they came into our universe billions of years ago.

These beings originate from a completely different universe and reside in higher dimensions and alternate realities, typically in the sixth to twelfth dimensions. However, most of them continue to exist as an exclusive group in the twelfth dimension. They are descended from tiny birds, and because they participated in the seeding of our universe, we can say that the birds on our planets are a gift from these enlightened ones.

Aside from having a greatly enhanced sense of consciousness, they can see the more abstract and expansive images of the entire multiverse and travel throughout the cosmos and consciousness through thought. They have a reputation for being able to communicate telepathically and mentally and have even created their own secret language. They carefully consider what worlds they will inhabit using this technique and then project themselves into the chosen world to establish themselves as resident lifeforms.

While their essence is incorporeal and spiritual, they can create physical bodies by projecting the cosmic energy that they normally use for communication through thought into the matter of a living planet.

The world's religions, theologies, mythologies, and histories all prominently feature the Avians' involvement in life on Earth. We find them in the descriptions of the Tetramorphs and the Cherubim in a variety of sacred texts from various religions.

The frequent mentions of creatures with human, lion, ox, and eagle-like faces reveal this. One passage from the Holy Bible that illustrates this is Ezekiel 10:14, which states, "Each of the cherubim had four faces: One face was that of a cherub, the second the face of a human being, the third the face of a lion, and the fourth the face of an eagle. In terms of Starseeds, we can draw some further interesting parallels between the lion and the reincarnated Lyran, the human beings and the Anunnaki, and the eagles and the Avians. Not only that, but all the way up to the book of Revelation, they can be repeatedly found, as in Revelation 4:7, which states, "The first living creature was like a lion, the second was like an ox, the third had a face like a man, and the fourth was like a flying eagle."

The eagle is one of the most iconic beasts in the book, serving as a sign of strength, power, vision, and even devastation. "But those who wait on the LORD shall renew their strength; they shall soar up with wings like eagles; they shall run and not be weary, and they shall walk and not faint," says Isaiah 40:31. This type of analogy may be found throughout the writings of Leviticus, Exodus, Deuteronomy, Proverbs, Job, and many more.

Even more intriguing is that this is a prevalent theme in most faiths, theologies, and myths stretching back to ancient Egypt and other ancient civilizations. The reference to winged creatures in the Bible is nearly identical to those found in the Egyptian pantheon in that many of them were humanoid with the faces of various birds of prey. This is represented in the Egyptian Gods and goddesses such as Ra, Horus, Thoth, Isis, and others. The ancient Egyptians also mummified millions of birds in Thoth's honor from 650 B.C. to 250 B.C.

The veneration of these sacred creatures also has relevance in Greek mythology, as seen by Zeus carrying a lightning bolt in one hand and a mighty Eagle extending its wings in the other. It is also evident in Mesopotamian mythology with Marduk's association with the eagle, symbolizing his power and authority. The Eagle was worshiped as a divinity in ancient Islam, and they even worshiped an Eagle statue. There are numerous allusions to the griffin, which has many similarities in

Persian myths and even in European, Anatolian, and many other cultures.

Avian Starseeds

According to estimates, there are only between 100 and 1000 of the Avian and Blue Avian Starseeds worldwide, making them the rarest group of Starseeds. They are a family of interdimensional heavenly entities that remain relatively mysterious to humans. Like other Starseeds, they have their own form of hierarchy, with the Blue Avian at the top.

Avian Starseeds are among the oldest sentient lifeforms in the cosmos, and they are unmatched in terms of creativity—perhaps only by the Starseeds from Lyra. As mentioned, they naturally function and live in the sixth through twelfth dimensions of the cosmos, a sharp contrast to civilizations like ours, which normally exist in the third to fifth dimensions. For this reason, they feel virtually stuck operating inside the boundaries of our 3-5D physical environment, which explains why there are so few of them on Earth. They've been here before and have come back with the same call for peace and to assist humanity in overcoming evil forces and the global ruling Cabal.

Avian Starseeds, some of the oldest souls in the multiverse, are innovative thinkers, which originates from their multidimensional view of cosmology. Their skills and talents are well known and documented across the universe, and they're also master astrologists.

The most essential things to the Avian Starseed are independence, sovereignty, and honor. They appreciate and honor all sentient lifeforms, regardless of shape, size, or color, and they demand the same in return. One of the worst things you can do to an Avian is to try to restrict them in any way. They are higher-dimensional beings that have transcended the dualism and physicality of our three-dimensional reality, and so they already feel uncomfortable in their bodies and third-dimensional environment. Denying them freedom and independence only increases their dread of being trapped.

Avian Starseeds, on average, have a sense of deep devotion to the Earth and the planet's people, but they also have a sense of right and wrong. They're well-versed in planetary affairs and care about the well-being of other sentient life forms and the global ecosystem. This is unlike humans, who are usually too self-centered to care about others.

Their skills and talents lie in the arts, religion, history, metaphysics, and the more spiritual aspects of our existence. Among their many contributions are their roles as guardians and protectors of sacred sites and artifacts and their service in maintaining the spiritual and astrological energy of the Earth. They are the ones who elevate vibrations at all levels of reality, from the individual to the cosmic. They are at the vanguard of expanding the boundaries of creativity and thinking and increasing the bar for developing greater levels of awareness, knowledge, and understanding.

Avians are here with a specific purpose: to bring about humanity's ascension to new levels of consciousness and awareness. They label their mission as the initiation of the Golden Age, which ultimately manifests as a global transformation of consciousness and humanity's transition into higher dimensions of universal evolution. They will bring into reality a new Earth by helping us rise above our current 3D existence into a new level of enlightenment through activating our dormant DNA codes, which hold all our potential for celestial divinity.

Characteristics of an Avian Starseed

- They are capable of seeing and understanding concepts that others cannot.
- They feel awkward being inside their bodies. They consider a 3D avatar extremely limited.
- They inspire humans to think bigger thoughts.
- They are acutely sensitive to colors, shapes, symbols, sounds, and vibrations.
- They have amazing memories and can recall any event or relationship with shocking clarity.
- They love the idea of bringing about a new Earth where they can experience freedom of thought and spiritual equality with all others from many different races, civilizations, religions, and creeds.
- They are masters at expanding consciousness through natural channels such as music, art, dance, conversations with others, different forms of meditation, and conscious breathing.
- They are obsessed with behavioral patterns. They can observe human behavior from many angles. A heightened state of

awareness gives them the unique ability to observe these patterns closely and extrapolate them into predictions about how a person will respond in different situations.
- They are here to aid the free-spirited who feel like they have been misled due to the domination and suppression of the masses. They often seek out many different ways of life and many different religions, lifestyles, and ideologies. Freedom of expression is their top priority because they simply know that all living beings are equal and have the divine potential to explore new realms of thought and consciousness throughout the cosmos.
- They possess incredible creativity, both a gift and a curse in this realm. In addition to being creative thinkers themselves, they recognize that creativity is an important tool in uncovering solutions for humanity's problems at this time.
- They abhor violence as well as ignorance and those who practice it. They believe everyone should be treated with respect, kindness, and friendship.
- They seek help from mentors within this dimension. They are not interested in worldly power or wealth, which they perceive as an illusion, because they know that the truth lies in the realm of the Spirit.

A Message for the Avian Starseed

Dear Avian Starseed, you are here to assist in the transition into the New Earth. You are here to help humans move into a higher state of consciousness. You are about to experience levels of freedom beyond anything you have ever known before. Be grateful for your experience on Earth because it has helped you develop the flexibility and wisdom necessary for moving into a New Earth.

You have worked hard on this planet, and now it is time to rest your body and mind as you enter higher-frequency realms of existence. The New Earth is a place of pure love and light, where you'll be surrounded by beings of elevated consciousness who are here to support you on your journey. You'll no longer be bound by the limitations of the physical world but will instead be able to tap into the infinite potential of the universe. Every part of your body is imbued with divine intelligence, and you are able to create the life you want simply by imagining it. What you most desire from this lifetime is accessible to you now that the veil has been lifted from your eyes. You can see the higher realms that await you—a state of existence beyond human imagination.

Chapter 13: Lemurian and Atlantean Starseeds

Geologists and biologists invented the term "Lemuria" towards the end of the nineteenth century to explain why lemurs may be found not only on the island of Madagascar but also on the Indian subcontinent and the Malaysian islands. A prehistoric land bridge connecting these now-separated places would explain how the lemur population managed to move from one site to the other—a feat that appears inconceivable if large amounts of water are thought to have been crossed. As a result, the hypothetical land bridge was dubbed "Lemuria." Its existence was determined in a manner similar to how fringe scientist Ignatius Loyola Donnelly deduced the presence of Atlantis, with lemurs acting as civilizations.

The works of theosophist Helena P. Blavatsky and her followers include the most sophisticated description of Mu/Lemuria. The Book of Dyzan, an old book, contains the real account of Atlantis and Lemuria, according to Blavatsky. Tibetan masters—teachers and practitioners of the age-old human arts—revealed this book to her. The Hidden Doctrine, a classic of theosophy, was released in 1888 and contains Blavatsky's interpretations and extrapolations of The Book of Dyzan. This doctrine claims that life developed on Earth in a series of phases.

In every one of these phases, mankind manifested in different shapes and with varying traits. Each stage is called a *"Root Race,"* and the history of mankind follows the progression of our species through seven stages, giving rise to seven Root Races. We are currently in the fifth stage, with the sixth and seventh stages looming in the distance, and each race is linked to a distinct continent.

The "Imperishable Holy Land" is where man's history began, according to Blavatsky. This Holy Land has never experienced the destiny of other rising and falling continents. It is said that it will exist from the beginning of time until the end of time. There have been claims that the Imperishable Holy Land is allegedly located at the North Pole, claims that may have looked more plausible in the 1880s than they do now. Others have speculated that this remote country is truly inside the earth and may be accessed through a large hole at the pole.

The North Pole – believed by some to be the "Imperishable Holy Land."
Christopher Michel, CC BY 3.0 <https://creativecommons.org/licenses/by/3.0>, *via Wikimedia Commons:* https://commons.wikimedia.org/wiki/File:The_North_Pole_(139653149).jpeg

W. Scott-Elliot, a supporter of Blavatsky, said in The Lost Lemuria (1904) that the First Root Race of the Imperishable Sacred Land had corporeal bodies made of "astral substance" that, if we could see them at all, would have appeared to us as enormous phantoms.

Blavatsky refers to the second continent as "Hyperborea." As the Second Race arrived, Hyperborea—which at the time included the entirety of what is now known as Northern Asia—stretched out its lands southward and westward to meet them. Since the planet had not yet tipped over on its axis, this northern continent is believed to have never experienced winter. While slightly more substantial than their ancestors, Scott-Elliot claimed that Hyperboreans were still essentially shapeless. They had simple skeletal and organ systems and underwent asexual budding reproduction, but they would have been invisible to the human eye, just like the First Root Race. The last remnants of this race, which eventually disintegrated, are found in the Arctic Circle.

The Third Race, the Lemurian, developed from the etheric Second Race. Even though their vertebrate structure had not yet solidified into bones like ours, their bodies had become material and were made up of the gasses, liquids, and solids that make up the three lowest divisions of the physical plane. At first, they could not stand upright with bones as malleable as those of young infants today, but in time, they acquired a sturdy bony structure around the middle of the Lemurian epoch. With their newly acquired bodies, Lemurians became more human-like. They developed a language, and their history and culture began on the Indian subcontinent.

The Atlantis continent was the fourth one. A Root Race that appeared completely human lived in Atlantis. Although most historians disregard the ancient record of Atlantis' existence, Blavatsky suggests that it should be considered the first historical continent. In The Story of Atlantis, Scott-Elliot provides thorough descriptions of Atlantean life and culture. Humanity first displayed cultural development, including literacy, the arts, science, and religion.

According to Scott-Elliot, the education provided to the exceptionally talented children of Atlantis included instruction in using psychic abilities and the occult healing powers of plants, metals, and precious stones. They learned how to harness the magical powers of the universe as well as the alchemical processes of matter transmutation. He talks about the amazing technological advancements made by the Atlanteans, such as flying machines and airships. The wealthy class intended to use these airships.

From two-seaters to ships with room for eight, they were typically constructed for a small number of people. However, these ships were employed in combat as the Atlantean age descended into warfare. These battleships were significantly bigger and could carry up to 100 sailors. They could travel at an elevation of several hundred feet and reach speeds of 100 miles per hour.

Unlike the earlier Lemurian Root Race, the Atlantean civilization contained organized religion. They held the concept of a Supreme Being represented by the sun. On hilltops where rings of upright monoliths were constructed, this sun-deity was worshiped. These monoliths, the surviving example of Stonehenge, were also used for astronomical rituals. As the end of Atlantis approached, the continent underwent a period of cultural degradation. Peace and prosperity led to strife and violence, and the sun's worship devolved into fetishism. The continent eventually sank beneath the ocean, and the once-great Atlantis was lost beneath the waves forever.

Atlantean and Lemurian Starseeds

These two ancient civilizations, now lost beneath the Earth's oceans, are said by some researchers to have left behind genetic and etheric DNA that is still a part of our collective consciousness. Also called Gaia Starseeds, they are the forefathers of our current civilization and continue to influence its destiny.

According to theosophists such as Alice Bailey, some Lemurian and Atlantean souls were advanced beings who achieved high levels of consciousness and now assist humanity from the unseen realms. They were thought to have originally lived in Atlantis and Lemuria but transcended to higher dimensions when these civilizations sank beneath the sea. Some of these souls were said to have incarnated on Earth in the 20th century and are alleged to have helped establish the New Age Movement and spread spiritual teachings.

These enlightened souls are believed to possess immense wisdom and knowledge, guiding humanity toward spiritual evolution and enlightenment. Through their subtle influence, they inspire people to explore their inner selves, embrace holistic healing practices, and seek unity with the divine. Lemurian and Atlantean Starseeds are seen as guardians of ancient wisdom, preserving esoteric teachings passed down through genetic coding. Their presence in the unseen realms serves as a reminder of humanity's potential for growth and transformation. As we navigate the complexities of modern life, their guidance offers solace and inspiration, reminding us to connect with our higher selves and embrace the interconnectedness of all beings. The legacy of these advanced beings continues to shape the spiritual landscape of our world, encouraging us to embark on a journey of self-discovery and transcendence.

Characteristics of Lemurian and Atlantean Starseeds

- **You Feel at Peace in or Around Water:** You feel at home near water, as if it holds a deep and profound significance for your soul. Whether it's the gentle lapping of waves against the shore or the tranquil flow of a river, being near water brings you a sense of calm and rejuvenation. You may find yourself drawn to bodies of water, seeking solace and clarity in their depths. This connection to water is a characteristic shared by both Lemurian and Atlantean Starseeds, as these ancient civilizations were deeply intertwined with the element of water. It is believed that Lemurians were highly skilled in harnessing the healing powers of water, using it for purification and spiritual growth. Similarly, Atlanteans were known for their advanced knowledge of underwater technologies and their ability to communicate with marine life. As a Starseed with these lineage connections, your affinity for water reminds you of your ancient origins and your innate ability to tap into its wisdom and energy.
- **You are Skilled in the Healing Arts:** It is believed that those Starseeds who originated from Atlantis or Lemuria inherited certain healing methods from their lineage. These ancient civilizations were known for their advanced scientific knowledge, and it is hypothesized that these techniques could have been passed down through generations of Starseeds, allowing them to harness the earth's energy and healing properties. As an Atlantean or Lemurian Starseed, you'll likely be talented in the spiritual healing arts, drawing on your ancestry's heritage to maximize your natural abilities. Some of the ancient Atlantean and Lemurian healing practices that may have been passed down to you include methods for purifying water and harnessing its energy for spiritual growth, the art of crystal healing, vibrationally-oriented therapies like reiki, and etheric energy manipulation.
- **You Are Sensitive to Nature:** Those who descended from the ancient civilizations of Lemuria and Atlantis are often deeply attuned to the energy of nature, possessing a powerful

connection with animals and plants. This sensitivity is likened to that of a psychic, allowing you to "feel" the presence of animals and plants around you. Your sensitivity is an innate talent that may have been cultivated in past lifetimes when Lemurians were known for their advanced psychic abilities and Atlanteans were renowned for their intuitive abilities. As a Starseed, your ability to connect with nature may cause you to develop into an accomplished healer and naturalist.

- **You Are Grounded:** You have a strong connection with the Earth and its chakras. Your essence is rooted and grounded in nature, so you are highly attuned to the planet's energy vibrations. You are often drawn to the natural world for inspiration and guidance, preferring to spend time outdoors in nature rather than indoors. Additionally, your personality may be highly influenced by Earth's energies, as some Starseeds born of these lineage connections are prone to experiencing life-changing revelations when spending time in nature.
- **You Have an Affinity for Crystals:** It is believed that in past lifetimes, Atlanteans and Lemurians were skilled in the art of crystal healing. This ancient healing practice emphasized the power of crystals to cleanse and revitalize human energy fields, restore health, and release negative energy. Lemurian Starseeds are often drawn to crystals for spiritual guidance and healing purposes and may be drawn to them as part of their metaphysical practice. The Lemurians' affinity with crystal healing dates back to their early Stone Age culture, when they used crystal power to cure illness, navigate the sea, and communicate with spirit guides.

A Message for the Lemurian and Atlantean Starseeds

Dear Lemurian and Atlantean Starseeds, you may experience a burning desire for spiritual evolution and expansion as you awaken to your divine purpose. You may feel drawn to explore your inner self through the healing arts, becoming a healer of substance and integrity. You are here to become an advocate for holistic healing practices, encouraging others to embrace the transformative power of nature for emotional and physical growth. As you continue down this path, be sure to incorporate both science and spirituality into your lifestyle, as these two principles have the potential for synergistic growth when balanced.

You may also find yourself drawn to water, with a deep connection likely passed down through genetic coding from Lemurian ancestors. Your ancestral lineage connections allow you to harness the element's energy for spiritual evolution and manifestation purposes. Water holds a profound healing energy that can be harnessed with the intentionality necessary to manifest your desires into reality. This deep connection gives you a wealth of inner guidance and wisdom, helping you cultivate your talents and manifest your dreams.

As you awaken to the truth within, you may remember a time when you mastered water-based arts in a culture that revered the power of the element. You may feel connected to this ancestral legacy, growing curious about your Lemurian or Atlantean origins. This is a sign that you are ready to tap into your soul purpose and expand your consciousness beyond the physical world's limitations. You are being called to become a force of healing and connection, bringing love and health to the world. When you embrace this calling, you'll spark a transformation of consciousness that can ripple through the planet, healing those around you and awakening them to their own divinity.

Chapter 14: Your Earthly Mission

This final chapter aims to guide Starseeds who are awakening to their planetary missions and challenges as they traverse the physical realms of Earthly life while remembering who they are. You need to remember, reconnect, and then discover the gifts you have been given to share with humanity. The world needs a shift in consciousness where we feel connected to each other again and can support each other with love, compassion, and patience. As a Starseed, you are here to assist in this shift. You may need to adjust your vibration at times, as the energies of this world can feel very heavy, dense, and difficult to handle. In fact, many Starseeds are on Earth for the first time and have no idea how to navigate their unique personalities and the challenges they face in their nascent earthly lives. As with any culture shock, there can be a sense of being overwhelmed and unsure of how to fit in. But here is the secret: You don't have to fit in. You can create and receive whatever you need to fulfill your mission. This is a beautiful thing. You can also choose not to accept any of the challenges you face. They can indeed feel substantial sometimes, but many times the lessons they teach you are what you need to reclaim your true self.

For you to become a successful Starseed, you need to find your purpose.
https://www.pexels.com/photo/notes-on-board-3782142/

As a Starseed, you are a consciousness of light and love. You are here to be a beacon of guidance for humanity, and the most delightful thing is that you won't have to deal with people who are not ready for the love that you give freely, which is unconditional. You are here to bless the earth and to uplift and assist humanity with your love, wisdom, and light. You are here to create beauty in the world. You can heal, restore, and replace what is not serving the universe in any way.

Remember that you are not alone and that you are being supported by the collective consciousness of Starseeds who have gone before you. Whatever your Starseed mission entails, some of the things you may experience include:

- Feeling overwhelmed by new and unfamiliar experiences all at once.
- Experiencing energy shifts, both positive and negative, within your body.
- Having a sense of déjà vu, knowing that you have been here before.
- Feeling disconnected from humanity and alien to the world you live in.
- Realizing that your life is not what it seems, and your soul mission is challenging your current reality.
- Feeling judged by others for the choices you make or the way you express yourself.
- You may feel confused about your purpose on Earth because things here are very different from where you have come from. You are a unique person, making it challenging to understand the ins and outs of human behavior and what is accepted as "normal" here on Earth.
- You may feel like you are seen as weird or different, or people may criticize the things you do. It helps to remember that what is weird and different here on Earth is special and unique elsewhere in the Cosmos.

Many Starseeds are being tested for their self-worth and self-empowerment. Being a pioneer of any kind is tough in this world where we have been conditioned to accept limiting beliefs about our worthiness by those who believe they have the right to manipulate others to their will for the sake of power, control, and greed.

Sometimes you feel emotionally, mentally, and physically overwhelmed by the world around you. The key to maintaining your sanity is to support yourself in ways that align with your gifts and talents. Make sure you are not sacrificing what brings joy into your life just because others say it is not "realistic, practical, or useful" in reality. This can be very challenging, but for you, it is all about being the shining light that you are. In this way, you are honoring your soul and your mission.

Protecting Your Energy Throughout Your Earthly Journey

Sometimes you may find yourself agitated by the people around you. You may feel like your purpose on Earth is being thwarted, or you may feel invisible and unheard. Things can be confusing, and sometimes you may feel very alone. As a Starseed, you are far more sensitive than most humans on Earth, as your consciousness has expanded in other worlds. You may find that emotions are more intense for you, especially negative ones like anger, fear, resentment, and sadness. The good news is that all these feelings will pass if you allow them to; they are not permanent fixtures in your life, even when they seem to be.

You must find ways to protect your energy from being manipulated by others. In this way, you can find the clarity of mind that you need to make sense of things so that your inner wisdom can guide you in the choices you make for yourself. To that end, these tips might help:

- Your first line of defense is your own mind. You have the power to control the thoughts you have. Understand that whatever you focus on, you attract more of it into your life. If you are worried, fearful, or anxious about a situation or people in your life, this thought energy doesn't serve you and will attract more situations that support these negative emotions. So, stay positive and focused on what brings light and love into your life.
- The next way to protect your energy is through meditation. You are already an expert in this art form, whether or not you realize it, so use it to guide you on the path of self-discovery and healing. Leave your mind open as you breathe in and out through your nose. As you do this, let everything you experience come and go without judgment or attachment. This allows your soul to connect with the present moment while also allowing it to send out loving energy into the world around you.
- Spend time in nature. This is one of the most grounding things you can do for yourself, as your energy will be lifted in the presence of trees, plants, and animals. Sunshine and fresh air also do wonders for raising your vibration.
- Surround yourself with supportive people who bring joy into your life. We all have relationships that no longer serve us, but

sometimes it's hard to let go of these people because we don't want to be alone. This is where you can use your intuition to discern if a person in your life is good for you or not. You know the answer when you feel good and happy in their company instead of feeling drained or confused.
- When going through difficult emotional situations, take care of yourself first; leave the drama for later. You may have to let go of certain people in your life to take this step.
- Connect with a healthy support system of friends who are also Starseeds. They will understand the unique challenges you face and will be an invaluable resource in helping you stay grounded and positive.
- Research the benefits of alternative healing methods for your body and soul. Many alternative methods can be very beneficial in helping you clear negative energy from your etheric field. This is one of the best ways to protect and replenish your energy.

Connecting with Other Starseeds

You may or may not have a difficult time making friends. If you do, it is likely because you are unique, and people are not always comfortable with those who are unlike them. You may find it easier to make friends with people similar to you regarding ideologies or interests. You should consider reading more about other Starseeds to connect with them and feel less alone as you navigate this strange and alien earthly journey. Here are some strategies that can help you find a connection with other Starseeds:

- Get in touch with other Starseeds on the internet. Many YouTubers, mediums, and authors have written about being a Starseed that you can follow and learn from.
- Join an alternative spirituality forum or class in your area. You can meet like-minded people and share ideas and experiences in these places.
- Attend a spiritual festival or retreat that celebrates the diversity of spiritual knowledge across astrology, mythology, magic, energy healing, meditation, divination, and many other areas of study.

- Share your experiences with loved ones who support you unconditionally without judgment or criticism, even if they don't understand what you're going through.
- Go to a psychic or medium who specializes in working with Starseeds and lightworkers. They can offer you guidance and support as you unpack your soul mission and the challenges you face in this dimension.
- Start writing about your experiences on the internet. If you're a writer, this is a great outlet for expression and helps keep your thoughts in check as you navigate this transition process. You never know; you may discover that others share your views and experiences and want to connect with you.

Being a Starseed is not always easy, but it is an honor to be incarnated at this time to help promote unity, consciousness, and positive change in the world. You know you're a Starseed when you feel like you don't belong and also have a deep longing for true connection with your soul group and fellow Starseeds who can help guide you on this journey of self-discovery. As a Starseed, your mission is to explore the depths of your soul to bring healing, peace, and unity consciousness to the world. This means having the courage to deal with your deepest fears and darkest emotions before you can rise into the light of truth, co-creating with people from all walks of life to make this world a better place. It's an exciting opportunity to be alive, so embrace your cosmic nature and take hold of your true power as a soul that has traveled many galaxies and dimensions. As you come into alignment with who you truly are, you'll discover that the experience of being a Starseed is one of empowerment and freedom—a path forward filled with endless possibility, adventure, and growth.

How to Identify Your Starseed Mission on Earth

The experiences that you go through during this lifetime are very specific to the mission that your soul group has agreed to come to Earth to work on. This will be the catalyst for your spiritual evolution. You may be leading a normal life when suddenly, an event or experience triggers the awakening of your Starseed memories. This can occur through karmic connections with people from other lifetimes who are now in your life, books you read, films you watch, or events you attend at spiritual gatherings, all of which hold the seed of awakening within them. You may not even be aware of the exact purpose of your life when you encounter this catalyst. However, the universe will continue to provide you with clues and opportunities to seek out the answers. Below are some signs that can indicate your Starseed mission on Earth:

1. Suppose you find yourself drawn to a subject or an area of study that you feel is too new or mysterious to understand. In that case, that's a sign that your soul has activated the intelligence of a new possible incarnation.
2. Suppose you feel unsatisfied with your current career path. In that case, no matter how much money you make or how beloved and famous you are, this is a sign that your mission demands that you move on from where you are.
3. Suppose you experience a sudden change in your relationships with people or acquaintances. In that case, this is a sign that you are being telepathically and energetically connected to someone from another lifetime in preparation for a karmic reunion.
4. If you begin to feel that a huge transformation is occurring within your life and you have no idea why, then this is a sign that you are being guided toward some type of karmic gift or hidden purpose in your life.
5. If an event or experience causes you to question your present reality, then this is a sign that the awareness of another lifetime has been activated within your consciousness.
6. Suppose you find that low-vibrational people are karmically connected to you. In that case, this is a sign that your mission is to awaken the Starseed in them through your own actions and words.
7. If you find yourself having vivid dreams or visions about somewhere unknown, yet feel an intense attraction toward the images in these dreams, then this is a sign that your soul memories are drawing on nature spirits from another lifetime to help with the activation of your soul's mission.
8. Suppose you feel that many people are moving away from your path or against your actions. In that case, this is also another sign that your mission requires you to raise the consciousness of other people.

9. If you find yourself being deliberately pushed into spiritual or personal development classes, books, or workshops by family, friends, or seemingly random people, even if you are very resistant to it, then this can be a sign that your mission requires that you take part in this event or activity.
10. Suppose people you meet for the first time tell you about spiritual books, experiences, or movies that resonate with your personal and spiritual growth. In that case, you are likely Starseeds who recognize each other. You could also have been brought together to support each other in a karmic situation.

Your mission is one of service and self-discovery on the path of awakening and empowerment. It is to embrace your cosmic nature and live with courage and passion, even in the face of ridicule or doubt from others. Your mission is to awaken humanity to their true stellar origins through your words and actions, teaching them about their multidimensional abilities while inspiring them to unlock the mystery of love within themselves. This is why fitting into earthly society, career paths, or relationships can also be difficult. However, the deep sense of longing you may feel as a Starseed is nothing more than a signal to awaken your mission. And it is important to remember that these feelings are not permanent or even real. These experiences are part of the catalyst that allows you to come to terms with the emotions that have been stored and suppressed within you, probably for lifetimes. The more you can open up and talk about your experiences, the quicker you'll be able to resolve them and move forward on your mission. Being a Starseed is a path of fearlessness, trust, and adventure. It is an opportunity to flow with the cosmos while awakening the Starseed within other people and yourself.

Conclusion

Starseeds are the masters of consciousness in our solar system. They have been working on this planet for a long time and are not even vaguely near finished. These loving beings are the keepers of light, and they work tirelessly to see that the light remains shining until every human being wakes up to the truth. One way they are connected to us is through the structures of mass consciousness that they have created on Earth, which we refer to as religions. They created these religious structures lifetimes ago to help raise the frequency of the planet and expand humanity's spiritual awareness.

Each religion offers a unique path toward enlightenment, catering to humanity's diverse needs and beliefs. From Christianity to Buddhism and Islam to Hinduism, these religions serve as guiding principles for millions seeking spiritual growth. Rituals, prayers, and teachings provide a framework for understanding the mysteries of existence and connecting with the divine. The celestial beings behind these religions understand that humans learn and evolve at different paces, so they have tailored each faith to suit various cultures and societies. This diversity allows for a rich tapestry of beliefs and practices that ultimately lead towards the same goal: awakening to our true nature as spiritual beings.

As we engage with these religious structures, we tap into the collective wisdom and energy of countless souls who have walked this path before us. We become part of a vast network of seekers united by our shared desire for truth and enlightenment. The universe continues to guide us through subtle whispers, synchronicities, and intuitive nudges, always inching us closer to the realization of our true selves. Through our beliefs and practices, we align ourselves with the divine and open ourselves up to the guidance and support of our galactic family. They assist us in our journey of self-discovery, gently guiding us toward a deeper understanding of our spiritual nature. With their help, we continue progressing towards awakening and enlightenment, constantly growing and evolving on our path.

Together with the collective wisdom of those who have come before us, we embark on a transformative journey toward the ultimate goal of union with the divine. This journey has its challenges as we confront our limitations and face the shadows within ourselves. However, with the guidance of the universe and the support of our spiritual community, we find the strength to overcome these obstacles and continue on our path of self-realization.

As humanity delves deeper into their spiritual practice, they will learn to cultivate qualities such as compassion, gratitude, and forgiveness. These virtues become the foundation of their interactions with others and shape their relationships with the world around them. They will recognize that every being is interconnected and that by extending love and kindness to all, they are contributing to the collective awakening of their species.

You can develop a heightened sense of awareness and a deep connection to the present moment through meditation and contemplation. You can learn to quiet the incessant chatter of your mind and tap into a profound stillness within. In this state of inner peace, you can easily access higher realms of consciousness and receive divine guidance.

The spiritual journey is not just about personal growth and enlightenment but also about spreading love and kindness to others. By recognizing the interconnectedness of all beings, we understand that our actions have ripple effects that can contribute to the rise or fall of humanity as a whole. Therefore, we must cultivate compassion and empathy, treating everyone with respect and understanding. As we navigate life, we encounter challenges and obstacles that test our strength and resilience. During these moments, we must remember to stay grounded in our spiritual practices, drawing upon the wisdom and guidance we have gained along the way.

By staying connected to our inner selves, we can find clarity amidst chaos and make decisions that align with our higher purpose. We continue to evolve and grow through self-reflection and introspection, shedding old patterns and beliefs that no longer serve us. This continuous process of transformation allows us to embody our true essence and live authentically. As we walk this spiritual path, we inspire others to embark on their own journey of self-discovery and awakening. Together, we create a collective consciousness rooted in love, compassion, and unity. Through this collective effort, we can bring about positive change and a new Earth.

Here's another book by Mari Silva that you might like

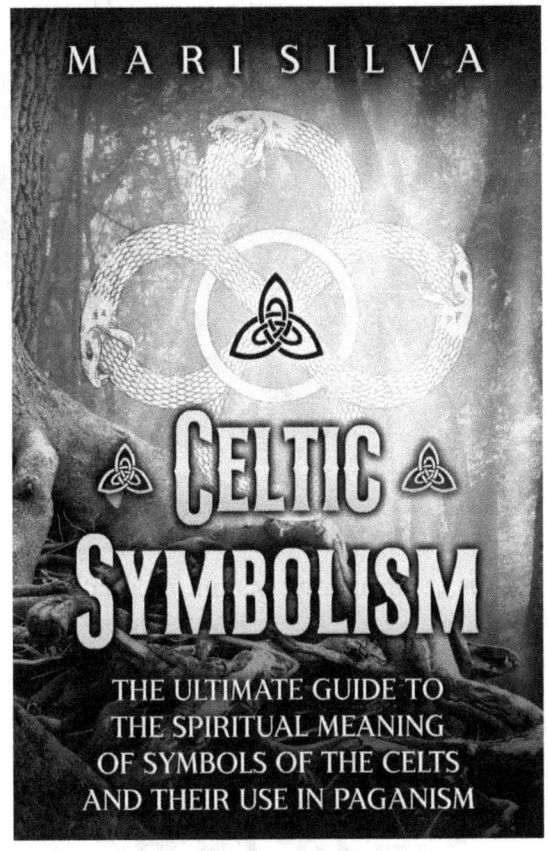

Your Free Gift
(only available for a limited time)

Thanks for getting this book! If you want to learn more about various spirituality topics, then join Mari Silva's community and get a free guided meditation MP3 for awakening your third eye. This guided meditation mp3 is designed to open and strengthen ones third eye so you can experience a higher state of consciousness. Simply visit the link below the image to get started.

https://spiritualityspot.com/meditation

Or, Scan the QR code!

References

Beaconsfield, H. (1998). Welcome to Planet Earth: A guide for walk-ins, Starseeds, and lightworkers of all varieties. Light Technology Publications.

Evans, W. J. (2021). Beginner's guide to Starseeds: Understanding star people and finding your own origins in the stars. Adams Media Corporation.

Fennell, A.-S. (2015). Starseeds of divine matrix. inspirational messages from enlightened beings. Lulu Press, Inc.

Gaughan, D. (2019). Star bred prophecy: A story of star people and Starseeds awakening. Independently Published.

Hoskins, R. S. (2012). For Starseeds: Healing the heart-pleiadian crystal meditations. Balboa Press.

Lanman, A. (2019). Conscious awakening: A research compendium for Starseeds wanderers and lightworkers. BookBaby.

Lewis, B. (2018). Star beings: Their mission and prophecy. Createspace Independent Publishing Platform.

Shaman, M. T., Pestano, M., Juan, A., Lopez, M., & Bliss, S. (2019). Awakening Starseeds: Shattering Illusions vol. 1. Independently Published.

Shurka, J., Finkel, L., Messner, S., Hopkins, P. W., & Seckinger, C. (2022). Awakening Starseeds: Dreaming into the future. Radhaa Publishing House.

Sim, G. (2019). Finding yourself for Starseeds and lightworkers: Activations from 7 star races for reawakening to your galactic presence. Independently Published

www.ingramcontent.com/pod-product-compliance
Lightning Source LLC
Chambersburg PA
CBHW072152200426
43209CB00052B/1155